IT Risk

Other Books in the Gartner, Inc./ Harvard Business School Press Series

*Heads Up: How to Anticipate Business Surprises
and Seize Opportunities First*
   by Kenneth G. McGee

The New CIO Leader: Setting the Agenda and Delivering Results
   by Marianne Broadbent and Ellen S. Kitzis

*Multisourcing: Moving Beyond Outsourcing
to Achieve Growth and Agility*
   by Linda Cohen and Allie Young

*IT and the East: How India and China Are Altering
the Future of Technology and Innovation*
   by James M. Popkin and Partha Iyengar

For more information on the series, please visit
www.gartnerbooks.com.

George Westerman
Richard Hunter

IT Risk

Turning Business Threats
into Competitive Advantage

Harvard Business School Press

Boston, Massachusetts

M C
Copyright 2007 George Westerman and Gartner, Inc.
All rights reserved
Printed in the United States of America
11 10 09 08 07   5 4 3 2 1

No part of this publication may be reproduced, stored in or introduced into
a retrieval system, or transmitted, in any form, or by any means (electronic,
mechanical, photocopying, recording, or otherwise), without the prior
permission of the publisher. Requests for permission should be directed to
permissions@hbsp.harvard.edu, or mailed to Permissions, Harvard Business
School Publishing, 60 Harvard Way, Boston, Massachusetts 02163.

Library of Congress Cataloging-in-Publication Data
Westerman, George, 1963-
  IT risk : turning business threats into competitive advantage / George
Westerman, Richard Hunter.
      p. cm.
  Includes bibliographical references.
  ISBN-13: 978-1-4221-0666-2 (hardcover : alk. paper)
  ISBN-10: 1-4221-0666-7
  1. Information technology—Management. 2. Management information
systems. 3. Risk management. 4. Information technology—Security measures.
I. Hunter, Richard, 1952- II. Title.
  HD30.2.W464 2007
  658.4'038—dc22

                                                        2007006516

The paper used in this publication meets the requirements of the American
National Standard for Permanence of Paper for Publications and Documents in
Libraries and Archives Z39.48-1992.

Contents

Preface and Acknowledgments

Writing a book about IT risk is like writing about life—the topic is so large and diverse that it's difficult to understand where to start, what to include, and how to say what we need to say. We decided to focus this book on a critical yet often overlooked issue: the link between IT risk management and business value.

No enterprise can be completely risk-free. Risk starts from the time someone decides to open the doors for business and doesn't end until the company is out of business. This includes IT risk, whose potential for harm has grown to the point that no business executive can afford to ignore it. Like any risk, IT risk is something to be managed, not eliminated. Managing IT risk is about making trade-offs between risk and return, between the risks a company can bear and the risks it would rather avoid. But, until now, business managers have lacked the tools to manage IT risk in these terms. We address that gap in this book.

This book is intended to help managers on both sides of the IT–business divide become comfortable making decisions about IT risk and ensuring that IT risk is being managed as it should. We have addressed the following questions: How can business executives understand the IT risks in their organizations? How can they work with IT executives to shape the enterprise's risk profile? How can IT and business executives build the capabilities needed to manage IT risk? And how can they together make informed trade-offs about the risks they face?

About the Research

This book is based on extensive research from the Center for Information Systems Research at MIT Sloan School of Management (MIT CISR) and from Gartner Executive Programs. The research investigates effective and ineffective approaches to managing IT risk. It provides a practical approach, illustrated by real-world examples, to understanding and managing the enterprise-level risks embedded in a firm's IT assets, processes, and people.

The research's foundations and insights come from these separate efforts, all led by one or both of the coauthors:

- An exploratory study conducted by George Westerman, including forty-nine interviews with CIOs and their counterparts in eleven enterprises. The study examined what constituted IT risk in these enterprises and what each was doing to manage IT risk. It generated the initial frameworks of risk and risk management capability on which our later research was based.

- Survey research with 134 firms, led by George Westerman and conducted through the auspices of Gartner Executive Programs. The survey enabled us to generate statistically based insights about the most important drivers of the four IT risks, as well as insights on what makes each risk management discipline effective.

- Case studies of nine firms—by Richard Hunter, George Westerman, and Dave Aron—as part of writing our first major report on the topic for Gartner Executive Programs, as well as many more developed through working with sponsors and clients. These helped refine our understandings and improve the practical insights of the research.

- Other case studies we have gathered over many years of managing, researching, and writing about related areas of IT management. These included experiences, interviews, and full-scale research studies related to major IT implementations, business agility, transforming legacy IT assets, CIO leadership, and other topics. Although we did not know at the time that these were about IT risk, they became highly relevant as we learned more about the way that risk management underpins nearly every aspect of managing IT.

- Executive presentations with more than two thousand IT and non-IT executives and middle managers. Their insightful comments and suggestions are an important and valuable source of testing, refining, and improving our ideas. Over the years we have been able to focus on the most useful ideas and concepts and make them practical for the real world of business.

Who Should Read This Book

This book is a useful source of ideas, insights, and examples for several different types of executives and managers from both business units and IT. Senior business executives and board members can use the ideas and frameworks to understand their role in managing IT risk and how they can perform this important oversight responsibility more effectively. CIOs can use the book to bridge the gap with business executives—making everyone more comfortable in managing IT risk—as well as to build the right risk management capabilities on both sides of the IT–business divide.

Specialized managers and executives can also use this book effectively. Business executives responsible for enterprise risk management, security, audit, or compliance will find valuable tools and examples to help them include IT risks in their risk management activities. Specialized executives—business unit chiefs to IT leaders in architecture, security, infrastructure services, application development, human resources, and relationship management—will find valuable ideas that can help them manage their risks and also clarify their roles in managing other enterprise risks. Finally, midlevel IT managers can use the book to develop a better understanding of the relation between IT and enterprise risks and how they can improve risk management capabilities or help shape their enterprise's risk profile.

Acknowledgments

So many people deserve thanks that it's hard to know where to start. First, we would like to thank the many executives who took the time to talk to us about how they manage their IT risks. Many people outside of MIT and Gartner—especially David Fachetti, Charles Gavin, Michael Harte, Robbie Higgens, Larry Loh, Kwafo Ofori-Boateng, Rick Omartian, Tom Prince, Patrick Purcell, Arne Skeide, and Karl Wachs—played essential roles in framing and interpreting the research and its implications, as did a few kind souls we cannot name for confidentiality reasons. We also would like to thank the many others who participated in interviews on risk or related topics, who completed our surveys, and who, upon seeing a presentation or report, offered valuable insights.

We would like to thank our colleagues for their continuous and unselfish support, advice, and assistance. George's colleagues at the Center for Information Systems Research at MIT Sloan School of Management—Julie Coiro, David Fitzgerald, Chris Foglia, Nils Fonstad, Chuck Gibson, Jack Rockart, Jeanne Ross, and Peter Weill—were always ready to provide advice, insights, or assistance when needed. Richard's colleagues at Gartner (including the Gartner Executive Programs research team, led by Mark McDonald, and Dave Aron, Diane Berry, Marcus Blosch, Barbara McNurlin, Patrick Meehan, Lily Mok, Tina Nunno, Andrew Rowsell-Jones, Chuck Tucker, and Andrew Walker) and the members of the Security and Privacy

Community and the Risk and Compliance Research Community (including Robert Akerley, Christian Byrnes, French Caldwell, Rick deLotto, Trish Jaffarian, Avivah Litan, Rich Mogull, John Pescatore, Romilly Powell, Paul Proctor, Donna Scott, and Roberta Witty) provided a wealth of research and review in support of our work here. We would also like to acknowledge the research assistance of several MIT master's students: Vikram Mahidar, Michele Salazar, Philip Sun, Robert Walpole, and Lenny Zeltser. Thanks also to Catherine Anderson, Jim Barrington, Brian Cleary, Chris Curran, Michael Duffy, Mike Flouton, Bud Mathaisel, Peter Morgan, Michael Schrage, and John Sviokla; and professors Ritu Agarwal, Cynthia Beath, Wynne Chin, Marco Iansiti, Blake Ives, Kalle Lyytinen, Warren McFarlan, Ryan Nelson, and Jeff Sampler for their advice and inputs on the research.

Finally, we would like to thank our friends and colleagues who helped make the writing process itself successful. Mark McDonald, Bob Yang, and three anonymous reviewers read early versions of the book and made important suggestions that helped shape the final product. David Fitzgerald, Jeanne Ross, and Peter Weill provided advice on the book-writing process, from proposal through to finished draft. And, finally, this book could never have happened without the expert input, encouragement, and management skills of editors Heather Levy, of Gartner, and Jacqueline Murphy, of Harvard Business School Press.

Personal Note from George

I would like to thank, first, my wife, Marilyn Augustyn. She is living proof to me of the message in this book: getting married may be a risk, but it returns tremendous value if you manage it well. Thanks for your love, tolerance, understanding, and help during the long hours of writing and rewriting (and every other time). Thanks also to my children, Henry and Clare, who brought new meaning to our lives and keep doing it every day. And thanks, finally, to my parents, sisters, friends, and mentors who have kept me on the right track, encouraged me in new things, and made it all enjoyable through the years. I am eternally grateful.

Personal Note from Richard

I would like to thank my wife, Patty; my children, Dean and Susan; my son-in-law, Jim; and my new grandchildren, Elias Hayes and Samuel Richard, for being the best and most wonderful people I know. We have all risked much and have been rewarded more often than not.

Introduction

IT Risk and Consequences

A HALF CENTURY of adopting information technology at an astonishingly rapid rate has created a world in which IT is not just widely present but pervasively, complexly interconnected inside and outside the enterprise. As enterprises' dependence and interdependence on IT have increased, the consequences of IT risk have increased as well. What is IT risk? It's the potential for an unplanned event involving a failure or misuse of IT to threaten an enterprise objective—and it is no longer confined to a company's IT department or data center. An IT risk incident has the potential to produce substantial business consequences that touch a wide range of stakeholders. In short, IT risk matters—now more than ever.

This change in the meaning and importance of IT risk has caught some executives unaware. Every executive at some time has experienced problems with his IT organization and systems, including delays and unexpected costs in development projects, temporary or extended loss of service, data loss or theft, processes made unnecessarily complex by systems interfaces and limitations, inaccurate information from redundant or "buggy" systems, and a myriad of other ills. Executives have generally learned to perceive—and even tolerate—such episodes as regrettably common but relatively limited in their impact on key business metrics. Case studies of companies like Tektronix and Comair, however, demonstrate how such perceptions no longer apply.

Comair, a $780 million subsidiary of Delta Air Lines, experienced a runaway IT risk incident on December 24, 2004, when the company's crew-scheduling system failed.[1] An airline's crew-scheduling system is mission critical. Federal Aviation Administration safety regulations limit the number of hours any aircrew member can work in a twenty-four-hour period. The scheduling system is what ensures compliance with that strictly enforced regulation. Without its scheduling system, an airline does not fly.

Because of the holidays, December is always the busiest month for U.S. airlines. December 2004 was busier than normal because unusually bad weather forced airlines to cancel or reschedule many flights, including 91 percent of all flights between December 22 and December 24. No one at Comair knew that the crew-scheduling system (which had been purchased from an external vendor) was capable of handling a maximum of only thirty-two thousand changes a month.[2] At about 10 p.m. on Christmas Eve, when Comair entered one more flight change, exceeding the monthly capacity, the system abruptly stopped functioning.

Comair technicians realized soon after, to their dismay, that the system could not simply be restarted. The only solution was to reload the entire system from scratch as quickly as possible. The tech team accomplished that task and relaunched the system late on December 25, but by then Comair had problems assembling its widely dispersed crews and aircraft where they were needed. The airline didn't resume normal operations until December 29.

As the company struggled to recover from the disaster, nearly two hundred thousand stranded Comair passengers helplessly roamed airport terminals throughout the United States. Airlines were fully booked for the holiday travel season, and there were few alternative flights. Throughout the Christmas holiday, camera crews from local and national television news outlets followed passengers through those terminals, broadcasting travelers' and Comair's distress to the American public.

Two weeks after the system failure, the U.S. Secretary of Transportation announced an investigation into the incident. A week later, the company's president, Randy Rademacher, resigned. In addition to the damage to the company's reputation, its management, and its customers, Comair's revenue losses as a direct result of this incident are estimated at about $20 million.[3] In other words, the loss from this single incident was nearly as high as the firm's entire $25.7 million operating profit for the previous quarter.

The company had planned, and delayed, replacement of the scheduling system several times before it failed.[4] Despite the outcome, these decisions could be defended as rational business decisions. The system had been running for years, and the likelihood of a complete system failure—especially one that resulted from an entirely unsuspected source—was apparently low. That the system failed at a point in time when its failure was maximally damaging to the company and its customers was extremely bad luck but hardly predictable.

But something more was involved than an unfortunate decision to defer an upgrade. Comair lacked a viable plan for the immediate recovery of this mission-critical business process. Its executives failed to plan for such a high-impact failure, however unlikely it seemed. When the software went down, there was no backup system that could be pressed into immediate service, no outsourcer on call and ready to step in, no plan that could keep the company running manually while the system was fixed.

In other words, it wasn't just the computer system that failed—it was Comair's process for understanding and managing the business consequences of IT risk. And making sure that an organization's major corporate risks—IT or otherwise—are managed to an acceptable level is the responsibility of the organization's senior executives. Perhaps that's why it was the company's president, not the CIO, who departed in the wake of the incident.

The Comair case is about the risk of *availability*. The Tektronix case is about *agility*—the ability to change rapidly with controlled cost and risk. In the mid-1990s, executives at the $1.8 billion electronics manufacturer learned that their plans to divest a major business unit had hit an unexpected snag.[5] Key financial and manufacturing processes for three Tektronix business units were riddled with undocumented interdependencies between critical systems. Extracting one business's systems from that tangled mass was like removing a load-bearing wall from a building—it couldn't be done without major restructuring. The separated unit would require duplicating nearly every one of Tektronix's major systems (including the sensitive corporate data they contained), as well as finding technicians to maintain the systems. The difficulty of spinning out a division, with or without its IT systems, brought a focus to those IT agility risks that had been present for years.

Tektronix arrived at this strategic dilemma gradually. For decades the company's IT department had extended existing systems, built new stand-alone systems, and written software to link systems as needed. Every new "solution" was an unconscious trade-off of long-term agility in favor of short-term benefits. The problems inherent in this approach weren't immediately apparent to executives, but they compounded over time, just as it takes time for unplanned, uncontrolled growth in a city to visibly overload roads, schools, sewers, and support services.

By the early 1990s, Tektronix executives knew their IT systems had problems. Changes took much longer to implement than they should have and than executives would have liked. It was frustratingly difficult to get an integrated view of the company's customers, products, and orders. Business managers complained that IT support was getting worse and worse, and IT managers knew that the systems were becoming more and more difficult to maintain. Extensive coordination by smart support staff covering for system inadequacies was so frequent that it produced a motto: "Five calls does it all."

But these ongoing signs of agility risks seemed relatively low impact. They were annoying, of course, but they were a more or less normal part of the way business was done at Tektronix and at many other companies. It was only when Tektronix executives tried to break from the past that they saw the real threat those familiar annoyances posed.

The Tektronix and Comair cases are extreme in their consequences, but they are not unique. Other events in multiple industry sectors show that executives must learn to think of IT risk in terms of serious business consequences:

- In mid-2005, CardSystems Solutions, Inc. reported that unknown persons had gained unauthorized access to computerized credit transactions for 40 million credit card holders. A few weeks after the breach, CardSystems' two largest customers, Visa and MasterCard, terminated their business with the company, which was soon after sold.[6]

- In 1996, a failed implementation of SAP's enterprise resource planning software at FoxMeyer, a $4 billion pharmaceutical distributor, allegedly led to the company's bankruptcy. The company's trustees filed suit against SAP (the software vendor) and Accenture (the systems integrator for the project), asking for $500 million in damages from each. The case was settled out of court in 2005.[7]

- In December 2003, the United Kingdom's Inland Revenue put a new system for managing tax credits into production. Preproduction testing had been limited to four weeks rather than the planned twenty weeks because the project was behind schedule. It is estimated that over £2 billion in erroneous tax credits were paid out by the system before errors were recognized and corrective measures taken.[8]

We could easily continue—there is no shortage of recent incidents of this sort, and more are reported every week. IT has become more and more central to business over the past twenty years, but many enterprises have not adjusted their processes for making key decisions about IT and IT risks. The result is risk incidents that have three factors in common:

1. They involve significant harm to constituencies inside and outside the enterprise that results from failure of IT systems or controls on IT processes.

2. Increasingly, they involve public disclosure, resulting in reputation damage and regulatory scrutiny.[9] Such public disclosure amplifies the consequences of IT risk, with subsequent consequences sometimes far exceeding the initial economic losses.

3. They expose failure to account for potential business consequences in managing IT risks—in other words, they expose a failure of general management, not just IT management.

Executives who invested—wisely—in IT as a strategic weapon simultaneously increased the IT risk to their enterprises. By depending more on IT for key processes, competitive efficiencies, and links to customers and suppliers, they increased their firms' dependence on smoothly functioning IT systems, as well as their vulnerability to external threats.

Many managers do not yet understand the full implications of this shift. To put it bluntly, management of IT risk has not kept pace with the reality of IT risk. IT risk in many enterprises is still handled as a technical issue and is largely ignored by business executives. Even when business executives understand the strategic importance of IT to their enterprises, they often have not been able or willing to make the hard trade-offs necessary to manage IT systems effectively.

The Causes of IT Risk

To understand what causes IT risk in organizations and how to manage it effectively, we undertook a set of research studies that combine academic rigor with the practical insights we have each gathered in over twenty years of working in and with IT organizations. More than 50 firms participated in case studies, and more than 130 firms participated in a survey associated with this endeavor. Executive presentations with more than two thousand IT and non-IT executives have helped us refine our research findings and relate them to real-world situations.

Our research shows that most IT risks arise not from technical or low-level people issues but from the failure of the enterprise's oversight and governance processes for IT. Such failures produce a series of poor decisions and badly structured IT assets that are manifested as ineffective IT governance, uncontrolled complexity, and inattention to risk.[10] In other words, most IT risk results not from technology itself but from decision-making processes that consciously or unconsciously ignore the full range of potential business consequences of IT risk. Over time, as risk-blind actions accumulate and compound, the conditions for disastrous, runaway risk incidents increase.

Ineffective IT Governance

Many of the risk factors we discuss throughout the book are symptoms of a common condition: a history of ineffective IT governance (see "What Is IT Governance?").

Inadequate IT governance—the absence of appropriate structures and processes for business involvement in IT investments and decisions—paves the path to risk in two important ways:

1. *Locally optimized decisions create enterprise risks.* IT organizations in many enterprises are organized and motivated (for example, through reporting lines and responsibilities) to be closer to the business organizations they serve and to respond to requests from the business as quickly as possible, rather than to take an enterprise view of IT decisions. Although each locally optimized decision may seem entirely justifiable and safe, the agility risks implicit in such decisions compound over time to dangerously high levels, as they did for Tektronix.

2. *Without business involvement, IT managers can make incorrect assumptions about which risks matter most to the business.* When markets, competitors, or corporate strategy change, the IT organization may learn slowly, if at all, that basic

---

What Is IT Governance?

IT governance is defined as "specifying the decision rights and accountability framework to encourage desirable behavior in using IT."[a] Just as in financial or corporate governance, IT governance is embedded in formal structures that allocate rights and responsibilities for decisions in certain IT domains (such as applications, architecture, and security) to appropriate business and IT executives. Governance decisions are supported by processes for surfacing information and driving resulting actions. In short, an IT governance arrangement describes how an enterprise's decisions related to IT are made and enforced.

a. Peter Weill and Jeanne Ross, *IT Governance: How Top Performers Manage IT Decisions Rights for Superior Results* (Boston: Harvard Business School Press, 2004), 2.

business assumptions and standard operating procedures must also change. The result is a gap between real and perceived risks and controls, leading to overinvestment in managing minor risks and underinvestment in more critical ones.

Effective IT governance is especially important in times of rapid strategic change, when previously valid assumptions about what matters most (and why) are questionable—and rapid strategic change is a fact of life in most industries today.

Uncontrolled Complexity

Complexity per se is not necessarily more risky than simplicity. Modern automobiles are much more complex than automobiles from the 1960s, but they are also generally safer, more reliable and efficient, and of far better quality overall. But complexity without solid engineering increases risk in many ways. Most important, complex environments that are not carefully engineered tend to be fragile. They have many moving parts, and the parts are prone to break or function unpredictably, with equally unpredictable effects on other business and technical systems. Such haphazardly complex environments demand a great deal of knowledge and attention to manage effectively, and those resources are scarce. The result is increased risk.

Inattention to Risk

Inattention to risk encourages operational risks. Symptoms of inattention include:

- *Missing or inadequate knowledge.* Layoffs, retiring personnel, promotions, and reliance on external consultants reduce an enterprise's core knowledge and open the door to risk.

- *Poor infrastructure management.* Inadequate device management and refusal to retire old, unreliable technologies lead to high costs and failure rates and to long recovery times.

- *Employee ignorance, negligence, or malfeasance.* Employees who do not know or care how to avoid risk and employees bent on destructive or criminal acts create failures and breakdowns of security and privacy.

- *Systems that are blind to dangerous activities.* Systems that fail to detect or prevent dangerous activities abet management inattention by removing a potential layer of automated warning and protection. Automated controls are particularly important when the enterprise allows key employees considerable authority to act autonomously. For example, appropriate levels of automated controls at Barings Bank might have detected the activities of Nick Leeson, whose unauthorized trades in violation of company rules lost $1 billion over nine months and bankrupted the institution.[11]

Ineffective governance, uncontrolled complexity, and inattention to risk create an environment of pervasive IT risk. Pervasive risks cannot be fully controlled by asking technicians to perform technical tasks differently. The risks are intrinsic to the way the company does business, not just to the way it manages IT. Further, risk factors reinforce and compound one another, so addressing individual risks that particular managers see does not address the full range of risks implicit in a given situation.

In short, having an excellent IT staff is not enough to control IT risk. Managing IT risk requires everybody involved to think differently. The CIO must make the business consequences of IT risk clear to business executives and provide a decision-making environment in which those executives can discuss and make decisions about IT risk in business terms. Business executives must ensure that the CIO has implemented risk management and must actively participate in the tough decisions and culture changes that IT risk management entails.

IT Risk as Business Risk and Business Value

Because IT risk is now business risk, with business consequences, enterprises must change the way they manage it. Businesses can no longer afford to assume that IT risks will be contained within the walls of the IT department, or even of the enterprise. They must replace technology-driven approaches and fragmented views of IT risk with an integrated view that starts with an understanding of the business risks and consequences that flow from IT decisions. Then they must take action.

This is essentially what Tektronix did after its rude awakening to IT risk in 1996. Led by the CFO and CIO, with strong support from the CEO, Tektronix redesigned its business processes and replaced its jumble of complex systems with an enterprise resource planning package. The initiative demanded committed leadership to make the case for change, convince skeptics to adopt standard processes, and discipline remaining holdouts. Not only did the information systems have to change—the undisciplined variety of business processes that produced the risk-ridden systems morass had to change as well.

The process was painful—it took three years and about $55 million to complete—but it was ultimately successful in many ways. Tektronix was at last able to acquire and divest divisions flexibly. The changes reduced other IT risks and improved business performance significantly as well. More accurate information, delivered faster, enabled higher inventory visibility, faster credit approvals, and a fivefold increase in the percentage of same-day shipments. In the end executives had better information to support strategic decisions, and more agility to implement those decisions.[12]

In our research we have encountered many companies that have turned around dangerously risky situations by building IT risk management capabilities incorporating two key elements:

1. They have adopted an integrated view of IT risk that allows them to make rational, informed trade-offs about IT risk in business terms.

2. They place careful emphasis on three core disciplines for managing risk: simplifying the IT foundation, creating a risk governance process, and fostering a risk-aware culture.

These elements work together. Without an effective risk management capability, enterprises cannot have useful conversations about IT risk. Without a common language that conveys IT risks in business terms, business executives cannot make informed decisions about these risks.

Managing an integrated business view of IT risk via the three core disciplines reduces IT threats while increasing business value derived from IT. If IT risk is handled as a compliance or avoidance issue, then it's just a cost to be managed. But if IT risk is handled in the right way, as business risk and capability, business value is created in three ways. First, there are fewer fires to fight, and the enterprise can focus on more productive activities. Second, the IT foundation is better structured and less costly, freeing resources for more productive activities. Third, the enterprise can pursue valuable opportunities that other firms would consider too risky to attempt.

Structure and Intended Readers of This Book

Many books have been written about specific elements of managing risk, in both business and IT. But, to our knowledge, this is the first book to provide rigorous research-driven advice and tools for building a comprehensive view of IT risk as business risk. As such, it should be read by business executives and IT executives alike.

If you're a business executive or board member, we provide ideas, frameworks, and advice to help you meet your fiduciary responsibility of managing IT risks as effectively as you manage other risks.

If you're an IT executive, we provide step-by-step advice and tools to help you build an IT risk management capability. We provide information in a practical form to help you start the program, find the right specialists for each element, and engage both business and IT people in the right roles.

Chapter 1 presents our key framework linking IT risk and business priorities. Contrary to the technical and compartmentalized way in which most enterprises manage IT risk, we argue that IT risks are best summarized in terms of four key business objectives: availability, access, accuracy, and agility. Technical risks can be best managed in terms of costs, benefits, and trade-offs among the business objectives—the same way executives make all their key decisions.

Finding a way to discuss IT risks in natural business terms is only the first part. Enterprises also must have the capability to identify, prioritize, and address the risks they face. Chapter 2 starts the enterprise on this path with a discussion of the three core disciplines of effective risk management:

1. A well-structured, well-managed *foundation* of IT assets, people, and supporting processes

2. A well-designed *risk governance process* to identify, prioritize, and track risks

3. A *risk-aware culture* in which people understand causes and solutions for IT risks and are comfortable discussing risk

Enterprises generally start with and emphasize one of these disciplines, but they must ultimately be capable in all of them. Over time, an enterprise may choose to change its emphasis as its capabilities mature.

Chapters 3–6 represent the heart of the book and offer a blueprint for developing effective risk management capabilities. These chapters have been written for IT executives, who will be responsible for implementing the practices, and should be skimmed by business executives, who will participate in the processes and charge their CIOs with implementing those processes. Chapters 3–4 describe how to improve the IT foundation of applications, infrastructure, people, processes, and controls. In these two chapters, we describe the IT risk pyramid and how executives can use it to manage the right risks in the right order.

Chapter 5 shows how to establish the second core discipline, the IT risk governance process. An effective IT risk governance process is coordinated by a risk officer, conducted by managers in each functional area, and overseen by executives at higher levels. The chapter includes processes and tools to make risk governance effective.

The final risk discipline, a risk-aware culture, is the topic of chapter 6. No process can be effective and no foundation can be protected if the enterprise is afraid to talk about risk. A risk-aware culture starts at the top with business executives who set direction, model risk-aware decision making, and reward effective risk management behaviors. The goal is a culture in which risk is discussed openly across the organization and actively managed to tolerable levels.

Chapters 7–9 bring the focus back to the business executives who are so critical to the success of IT risk management. IT risk has serious business consequences, and business executives have important roles to play in managing IT risk effectively.

Chapter 7 describes how to assess each discipline—the foundation, risk governance process, and risk-aware culture—in your organization and bring each up to at least a competent level. Although enterprises must become competent in all three disciplines as fast as possible, they often choose one focal discipline as the rallying point to continuously improve all three well beyond the competent stage.

We present diagnostic tools to assess the pros and cons of different focal discipline choices in your organization.

Chapter 8 is about looking forward to anticipate strategic risks. Much risk management is about identifying and resolving risks in the present or near future, but executives have a duty to make sure that the enterprise is viable for the long term. Accordingly, in this chapter we describe how to incorporate risk management into the firm's considerations of likely future strategic changes.

Chapter 9 concludes the book with a summary of key themes and an executive call to action. It highlights the ten ways executives can improve their IT risk management.

One

The 4A Risk Management Framework

I N THE EARLY DAYS of the Internet, the IT group of an insurance firm had responsibility for hosting and maintaining the firm's newly developed Web sites. The IT team provided on-site support sixteen hours per day and was on call after hours. Everything was going smoothly, or so the IT team thought—but it was not long before a senior executive in one division demanded that support for the Web sites be outsourced. In rebuttal, the IT team prepared a full analysis of internal and external services and recommended that outsourcing be deferred. In the team's opinion, internal staff could provide cheaper, more responsive support for the sites during their sixteen hours of full coverage, and they wouldn't charge extra for unexpected changes or new Web pages. The company's traditional service channels were still available if a site went down, and an on-call technician could fix any problem within two hours, if that were really necessary. The IT team had long been schooled by management to keep costs as low as possible. The big risk, in the team members' opinion (and as customary for the company), was overspending on a new, unproven technology.

To the IT team members' surprise, their recommendation was rejected. To them, the Internet was nothing more than a new technology, but to the business, it was a strategic new service channel with very new rules—a symbol of the firm's innovativeness and willingness to go the extra mile to provide high-quality service. The business's idea of unacceptable risk was a minute of unplanned downtime because it had the potential to damage the dramatic service delivery and customer satisfaction improvements that its Web strategy promised. A little extra expense to ensure continuous uptime was hardly significant compared to the potential opportunity costs of downtime.

In a different case, the new CIO of a chemical company, looking for budget cuts, noticed that his predecessor had negotiated a costly guarantee with the firm's IT-outsourcing vendor. The company's order processing, accounting, and shipping systems would be restored within fifteen minutes in the event of failure. The CIO wondered why. "A fifteen-minute recovery is critically important for banks," he thought, "but we're a chemical company! Most orders could be delayed for hours without any impact on our customers. Why are we paying a premium for a fifteen-minute guarantee on these systems?" The company's senior management team agreed with him that the costs were high relative to the business risks. The company soon after traded its expensive near-instant recovery plan for a guarantee of recovery within twelve hours, at an annual savings of 3 percent of the IT budget—more than enough to compensate for the risk that an order might be delayed to the point that a customer would notice.

As these examples show, it's difficult in many enterprises for business and IT people to exchange information about IT risks in a mutually enlightening way. The specialized language and worldview of IT are very different from the issues that concern a general manager or other top executive, and managers must take steps to bridge the gap.[1] The prior CIO of the chemical company, thinking in terms of personal and technical risk, overinvested to ensure that IT would never cause a business process to fail; the new CIO, thinking like a business executive, saw IT risk as a condition to be managed using the same kinds of business trade-offs that the company's executives made every day.

The business perspective is essential when it comes to understanding the consequences of IT risk. To make effective trade-offs about IT risk, a business executive needs to know what happens to the business when technology fails or underperforms. For example, in the specific case of availability risk, if a system is out of commission for two hours, how many orders will be lost or not shipped? Which employees will be idled? Who will be paid incorrectly or not at all? Which customers will be disappointed or angered? What market, legal, or regulatory costs will be incurred, and what opportunities deferred or lost? What alternative means of doing business are available, and what are their limitations? How do these specific availability risks trade off against other risks? Until those questions are answered, the failure of the system is only a circumstance that may or may not be a problem worthy of attention and resources.

A Holistic View of IT Risk

Executives who don't understand the business implications of IT risk chafe at what they see as unreasonable restrictions on their freedom to act and at the apparent inability of IT personnel to understand the importance of moving quickly to seize market opportunities. IT personnel, on the other hand, faced with the difficulty of keeping a complex technological platform running smoothly, don't always consider the business implications of their technical decisions. In fact, many

IT organizations are structured according to technical risk factors—the infrastructure group, the application development groups, the vendor management group, and so on. These groups address risks in their own technology silos as best they can. But they may be guided by out-of-date assumptions about business priorities or unduly influenced by the internal customers who shout loudest. Ultimately, these groups often fall back on what they know best: that it's their job to make the technology work—period—and anything that gets in the way of that mission is an intolerable risk. Decisions are rarely made holistically across the different types of risk factors. But the holistic view is exactly what's needed.

Just as IT risks have business consequences, managing IT risks has implications for the ways business is done. IT risk management solutions that don't take business needs and practices into account may be technically correct, but they're generally insufficient. The reverse is also true: business staff who don't factor IT in can't be sure that the resources necessary to contain business risks will be there when they're needed. (See "Making Business Decisions About IT Risk at Novartis.")

Consider the disaster recovery plan created by the IT group in a *Fortune* 500 financial services firm. The plan ensured that in the event of an earthquake, flood, or other unforeseen event that destroyed company headquarters, the IT group would have critical systems up and running at a backup site within thirty minutes. It was an impressively detailed plan, but it didn't solve the real problem, which was to get the *business*, not just the systems, functioning again. IT staff was unable to get the time and support of business experts to complete that part of the plan. And so matters stood until the IT team pushed the issue by conducting a highly visible test of one of the disaster scenarios. The test made it abundantly clear that even if the IT systems were working within thirty minutes at the backup site, business could not be done without adequate office space, furniture, telephones, and other supporting business infrastructure. With the real gravity of the situation starkly evident, business

Making Business Decisions About IT Risk at Novartis

CIO Jim Barrington leads IT for Novartis, a $37 billion company with over one hundred thousand employees. To him, a business-risk-based approach is essential: "The organization is so complex, with seventy-five thousand PCs, thousands of servers, and all sorts of security requirements. You can't manage all of the risk associated with such a large environment in a perfect way. We've taken the approach that if we can't eliminate the risk, we'd better try and understand and manage it.

"We've started looking at the business risk associated with this server going down, this application not being available, not getting Sarbanes-Oxley compliance, and so on. Once we know the risk, we try and manage the solution or the effort in direct relation to the size of the risk. For example, it probably doesn't matter if one of our payroll systems breaks. We can give people cash; we'll give them checks. It's no business risk whatsoever. Consequently, we shouldn't spend fortunes in having backup data centers to duplicate all that. But clinical trial data coming from research studies involving hundreds of patients is vital. This stuff cannot be reproduced easily. There's a huge risk to the business if we would lose it—financial, reputation, all types of things. As a result, we implement extremely robust security to protect, back up, and secure this data.

"So we're now focusing our resources in direct relation to the size of the perceived risk. And that's very helpful for us. We don't have to do everything for everybody in the same way. We get rather more focused, and of course then we get a much better leverage on our resources: people, time, and money."

Source: Jim Barrington, interview by George Westerman, from "IT Risk Management: Four CIO Vignettes," video (Cambridge, MA: Center for Information Systems Research, MIT Sloan School of Management, 2005). Used with permission.

managers agreed to help complete and manage the plan for business recovery.

The mirror image of this case is the customer service manager in a utility company who made detailed plans for emergency backup office space in the event of a disaster but forgot to make arrangements for power, phone, and network connections sufficient to support customer service staff and their computers. Fortunately, for all concerned in that case, the backup facilities could be wired to do the job. But that was just luck, and no one needs to rely on luck to manage IT risk. Tools are available to eliminate the miscommunication that increases IT risk and its business consequences.

The 4A Framework

We developed the 4A framework as a mechanism for translating IT risk into business terms. The framework defines IT risk as the potential for an unplanned event involving IT to threaten any of four interrelated enterprise objectives: availability, access, accuracy, and agility, as shown in table 1-1.[2]

The 4A framework begins with the understanding that every IT risk has business implications that involve trade-offs among different business risks or objectives. Any IT risk, therefore, must be understood in terms of its potential to affect *all* of those enterprise objectives that are enabled by IT. These objectives are concisely described by the 4A framework.[3]

Thinking in terms of the 4A framework allows business and IT personnel to discuss IT risks in the same terms and to develop a mutual, integrated understanding of the business consequences of IT risk, and how to address the risks. Executives make risky decisions every day to seize opportunities and avoid dangers. But they are rightly wary of risky decisions when they don't know enough about the issue to make an educated guess. Regardless of how much technical information they're given, many executives don't feel they have enough knowledge and instincts about technology to make competent decisions. They often don't even know what questions to ask of the IT team. Putting IT risk into business terms means that the conversation is about things executives know intimately. They know what an hour of downtime means in the factory and can compare it to the impact of an hour of downtime in the HR systems. They can compare the value of better internal access to data to the potential losses that might result from leaking sensitive information. They can understand how accuracy issues impede decision making, destroy supply chain efficiencies, and pose a regulatory threat for Sarbanes-Oxley. They can assess the impacts of a delay in a major strategic change initiative better than anyone else in the organization.

With the potential costs of IT risks defined in business terms, everything is clearer. The IT team can provide useful input to decision making via scenarios with different cost and risk implications, and businesspeople can choose between alternatives whose upsides and downsides they understand.

TABLE 1-1

The 4A framework for managing IT risk

Availability Keep the systems (and their business processes) running, and recover from interruptions.

Access Ensure appropriate access to data and systems so that the right people have the access they need and the wrong people don't. (The potential for misuse of sensitive information falls in this category.)

Accuracy Provide correct, timely, and complete information that meets the requirements of management, staff, customers, suppliers, and regulators.

Agility Possess the capability to change with managed cost and speed—for example, by acquiring a firm, completing a major business process redesign, or launching a new product/service. (IT conditions that narrow enterprise options for action fall in this category.)

Source: © 2007 MIT Sloan Center for Information Systems Research and Gartner, Inc. This material is adapted from a framework originally developed in George Westerman, "Understanding the Enterprise's IT Risk Profile," Research Briefing IV(1C) (Cambridge, MA: Center for Information Systems Research, MIT Sloan School of Management, March 2004). Used with permission.

The Tektronix case described in the introduction is a striking example.[4] The costs of change were high, and so were the risks. A $55 million dollar enterprise resource planning (ERP) project spread over three years is not a trivial investment in time, attention, and resources, even if the project comes in on time and on budget. But the business case for change was very clear. If the project failed completely, Tektronix would lose $55 million and whatever opportunities it had forgone to fund and staff the project. If the project succeeded, the company would eliminate a serious, proven threat to agility that had already prevented the sale of a division and that would continue to put strategic constraints on the company going forward. Further, success would reduce nagging accuracy risks— such as inadequate global views of customers, overly slow credit approvals, and spotty visibility of inventories outside the manufacturing plants—that constrained effective operations and damaged the company's relationships with customers and suppliers. The project was not an investment in IT; it was an investment in the continued viability of the business. The project risks were manageable; the risks of the status quo were not.

Using the 4A's to Guide IT Risk Management

In table 1-2 we discuss a sample set of questions based on the 4A's that will help senior executives start to meet their responsibility for overseeing IT risk. These questions aim to help executives build better awareness of risk-related conditions and deeper insights into how risk tolerance should vary across the firm, and to help IT managers build the required risk management capabilities. By revisiting these questions periodically, business executives can identify high-level changes in operations or strategy that change the organization's relative risk tolerance.

TABLE 1-2

Executive-level questions about the 4A's

Business executives can set direction for the enterprise's IT risk management efforts by discussing a set of high-level questions on each of the 4A's. The goal is not to talk for hours about each detail, but rather to discuss the most important items and the relative risk tolerances across units, processes, and each of the A's.

To start the ball rolling, senior executives can consider risks related to *availability*:

- Which of our major processes (e.g., customer order processing, manufacturing, supply chain, distribution, engineering design, HR self-service, accounting) are most dependent on IT, and what consequences (in terms of revenue loss, customer or supplier relationships, regulatory action, reputation, and other business impacts) are likely if the supporting systems are unavailable?

- Given that assessment, which processes and systems have the highest business priority for recovery in the event of failure?

Access questions focus on the value of information and the consequences for its misuse:

- What broad categories of information (such as customer credit card information, health-care records, product designs, employee e-mails, business plans and strategies, contracts, internal financials, inventories, and HR and benefits information) are most critical to the success or failure of the organization?

- What consequences (in terms of revenue; customer, supplier, or employee relationships; regulatory action; reputation; etc.) are likely if information in a given category is inadvertently released, lost, or compromised?

- In contrast, what broad categories of information would cause little damage to the firm's business or reputation if mishandled?

Accuracy-related questions for senior management's discussions focus on the impact of incomplete and inaccurate information on strategies and decisions:

- For key processes or categories of information, is data sufficiently accurate and timely to satisfy internal and external requirements?

- What constraints has incomplete or inaccurate information imposed on the organization and its plans?

- Which processes and categories of information carry the highest consequences for inaccuracy (in terms of revenue; customer, supplier or employee relationships; regulatory action; reputation; etc.)?

- What processes could benefit by having more complete information, such as a single global view of a customer, global view of the supply chain, or integrated product-level sales information across sites? How?

Finally, consider *agility*-related questions:

- How often do business projects with significant IT involvement come in on time and on budget? Do they deliver expected business benefits? What are the business consequences of project failure or delay (in terms of revenues, customer and supplier relationships, regulatory action, etc.)?

- What major strategic changes (new product launches, new geographies, mergers and acquisitions, global cost cutting, etc.) are foreseeable, and how well can IT support them? What kinds of strategic moves will be very difficult for IT systems and staff to handle, and how likely are those changes to happen?

Discussions of these questions in the senior management team should aim for informed breadth rather than extreme depth. Each business executive should take her own perspective as head of an important part of the business, but then compare answers across the team. Do the answers agree? Do some processes or units have more risks than others or more tolerance for certain risks than others? Are there any glaring inconsistencies or holes that must be addressed immediately?

The CIO should be part of the conversation, but this is fundamentally a business conversation about business priorities, not a technical discussion. The CIO can guide the discussion and answer questions when necessary. The CIO might even prepare initial assessments in advance for consideration in the meeting. But business executives should make an effort to address each question personally for their areas of responsibility.

At the senior executive level, it's enough at the start to define which risks matter most and why. Discussing the relative importance of IT risks and consequences to enterprise goals provides general direction on the enterprise's risk tolerance across units, processes, and each of the A's, and may generate an initial list of major IT risks. The information from these discussions is passed down the line to operational managers for more detailed assessment and action.

Table 1-3 provides a sample of follow-up questions operational managers in IT and the business can use to assess how well the firm's IT systems, people, and management processes match the desired enterprise risk profile. We do not mean to imply here that operational managers should be encouraged only to assess and act on risks and priorities that are passed down from the executive team. An important IT risk may appear at any level of the enterprise, and no manager should ignore such risks just because they don't appear on a prioritized list from a senior executive. Our point is simply that operational managers will be able to make better decisions about IT risks—and to avoid numerous arguments about priorities—when they understand which risks are considered most important by the

TABLE 1-3

Operational-level questions on the 4A's

After executives answer high-level business questions about the 4A's (see table 1-2), operational managers (both business and IT) can examine how well IT assets, people, and processes deliver on the direction. In the process, they will identify gaps that need to be filled and priorities that need to be changed so that the firm's IT risk profile can start to match the executives' priorities.

A few sample follow-up questions for operational managers in each category include:

Availability

- For the most critical processes and systems, exactly how long can we operate without the systems before intolerable consequences occur?
- How likely is a major disruption to these systems from internal or external factors (such as weather, a regional power outage, a natural disaster, age, and technical quality, or the lack of a vendor or internal support)?
- Do we have backups, recovery sites, manual workarounds, or other effective means of reducing the potential for loss of availability in these systems?
- Are early warning signs of failure already present in any processes (such as frequent outages, a major recent outage, or significant changes in external factors that can produce failure)?

Access

- Are there signs that current protections for our most sensitive types of information may be less than adequate? Have recent breaches occurred? If so, under what circumstances?
- Do employees have access to enough information to do their jobs? Do they have access to more information than they need?
- How do we ensure that our external partners, vendors, and contractors are protecting access as well as we would like them to? Do contracts specify how access information, user IDs, and passwords will be protected?
- Are procedures in place to remove access immediately when relationships end?

Accuracy

- What are the risk/benefit/cost trade-offs for both internal and external stakeholders (such as managers, employees, suppliers, customers, and regulators) of providing (or not providing) integrated information for processes that currently lack such information?
- What are the biggest nonsystem sources of data inaccuracy or inconsistency (such as skills, manual data reentry, unwieldy identifiers, lack of verification for data entry, etc.)?
- What relatively simple changes to internal controls, automation, or management procedures could reduce accuracy issues?

Agility

- How well does the IT organization's project delivery capability support the needs of each business unit? If there are differences in perception across units, is it due to different IT capabilities, different business-unit-based IT organizations, different needs, or some other reason?
- How can the track record for delivery be improved?
- What initiatives are needed to reduce the difficulty of projected strategic changes?

leadership team and why. The 4A framework helps executives and managers ensure that their understanding of the meaning, potential consequences, and relative importance of IT risks is as complete as possible and that guidance to managers at lower levels is considered and clear.

Decisions about which risks matter most, and why, are always specific to the enterprise. Consider, for example, the IT risk rated most important in late 2004 by the senior team of Barnardo's, the United Kingdom's largest children's charity: the potential for unauthorized access to, or compromise of, information about Barnardo's child clients and donors.[5] Such an incident would not be catastrophic for many businesses, but it could easily be for this one. Misuse of client or donor information could cause great harm to Barnardo's reputation. Without a spotless reputation the charity can't raise money, and without money it can't carry out its mission to serve children in need. The biggest IT driver of reputation loss for Barnardo's is *access risk*: the possibility that the wrong people will gain access to private information about Barnardo's clients or donors. Failures in availability, accuracy, and agility might have serious consequences, but none of these, unlike an access incident, could produce a catastrophic business failure quickly and without warning.

Using the 4A Framework to Analyze Risk Trade-offs

Analyzing risks in terms of the 4A framework makes it easier to allocate investments to shape a risk profile that's right for the enterprise. Without such a mechanism, there's as much danger of overinvestment in risk management as there is underinvestment. Let's look at a few examples.

Example 1: Buying a Nonstandard Package

Suppose that a business unit in your company wants to buy a certain software package that doesn't fit internal technology architecture standards. Another package is available and it's compliant with standards and generally adequate for the business purpose, but its features and functions will require some changes in business process and practices.

This is traditionally a terrific setup for a battle. If the argument is basically about the importance of following technology standards and your company is like most, IT will simply lose. If the argument is instead about weighing different business risks, the business can make a much better informed decision.

A nonstandard package carries potential risks in terms of access (how do we integrate it with our security processes, and what happens if we don't?); availability (who will support it, and how much downtime is acceptable?); accuracy (can we easily integrate the data this system produces with our financial and manufacturing systems?); and agility (will it impact our ability to roll out standard business processes with robust systems support, and can we modify the system easily when our business model changes?)—each of which has business consequences in terms of total cost of ownership, compliance with regulators and Wall Street demands, and so on. Against these, the business can weigh the risks of the process changes that the alternative will require (what happens if we have to do things differently, and do the things we'd have to give up really add value?). The decision may still be the same in the end, but either way the people involved will know what they're really getting—and what they're really paying.

Example 2: Merging Systems

A merger or acquisition is a similar situation on a larger scale and another case in which implicit IT risks are better defined and discussed as explicit business risks. It's expensive and demanding to convert an acquired company's systems to the acquirer's systems and processes. But depending on the strategic intent behind the merger, full integration may offer lower IT risks and business consequences in the medium to long term. Integrating and standardizing on a common set of technologies and processes reduces availability and access risks because IT has only one set of technologies to manage. Accuracy risks are reduced when numbers are generated in a common way and integrated automatically. Even agility risk is reduced in the long term because the standardized technology is less difficult to change, costs are lower, IT-based synergies are more easily attained, and it's easier to sell or spin off business units. All this explains why one global auto parts manufacturer immediately replaces the systems of the companies it acquires with its own standard ERP configuration, further reducing accuracy and agility risk by simply converting the last set of numbers (but not the entire history) from the acquired company's systems to the new standard.

Example 3: Rapid Growth Versus Control

Rapidly growing companies often take shortcuts with their IT controls and standards to introduce new processes and applications as quickly as possible. Time-to-market pressures require such firms to quickly launch new functionality regardless of efficiency, integration with other services, or potential for leverage via reuse. For them, it's more important to seize the next opportunity than to have well-controlled, efficient IT assets. In other words, they're more afraid of threats to agility than threats to access or accuracy.

But inadequate controls and management processes create fresh risks over time. Access risks increase as passwords proliferate and systems become intertwined in complex, undocumented ways. Accuracy risks increase because information is defined in different ways in different systems. Even agility risk increases because applications grow resistant to change as their complexity and interactions increase and their documentation declines. At some point—usually when complexity begins to visibly constrain the business—the rapidly growing firm finds that it needs to revisit the trade-off between agility and the other risks.

This is exactly what happened to Manheim Interactive, the online business unit of Manheim Auctions, the country's leading vehicle remarketer.[6] During the high-growth years after Manheim launched its online services in 1996, its focus was on speed of delivering and enhancing new services. The goal was to implement new business initiatives as rapidly as possible without becoming bogged down in formal management processes that could get in the way of agility. By 2000, however, IT managers began to see that the focus on speed was becoming unsustainable. The director of software development recalled, "The ability to always respond quickly eventually became a problem. We became very good at scrambling to meet demands very quickly, but that has a cost and eventually we just said, 'Okay, we're out of magic dust now. We need to rethink.'"[7] Manheim formalized its software development process, added a quality assurance staff, and defined clear responsibilities in each project for the product management, development, and quality assurance groups.

Using the 4A's to Resolve Disagreements over Unspoken Assumptions

As these examples show, there are no correct answers to how trade-offs between availability, access, accuracy, and agility risks should be made; the answers change over time with strategy and circumstances. Executives can't apply a simple formula; they can only make informed decisions. But the same can be said of every decision an executive makes about market risk, credit risk, or opportunity risk. The key is balance. By putting IT risk in business terms, the 4A framework lets businesspeople balance trade-offs among IT risks just as they do for all other business risks. It also helps managers get to the heart of disagreements that are founded on differing assumptions about risks.

The case of Virtual Services, Inc. (VSI) offers an example of how one company resolved a difficult impasse over an IT initiative by surfacing hidden assumptions about the relative importance of each of the 4A's.[8] You have probably seen advertisements on telephone poles or in magazines that entice people to earn money in their spare time by working from home. One of the companies behind those ads is VSI, a small firm that specializes in medical transcriptions. Through these and other advertising methods, VSI built a virtual workforce of part-time and full-time people. VSI trained these home-based workers to log into the firm's proprietary system, download doctors' voice recordings, and upload completed transcripts. The business model made efficient use of the workforce's time and VSI's systems, and the systems protected the confidentiality of the transcripts. With its IT systems and well-trained virtual workforce, the company could guarantee reliability, speed, and high privacy standards for its clients.

The business model was remarkably effective and efficient. Over six years, the firm grew to three thousand employees and $130 million in revenues. But by then the company was on the verge of outgrowing the capabilities of its systems. The CIO proposed a new system based on secure private lines, remote access servers, and proprietary technologies—all of which were highly reliable and virtually bulletproof. But the CFO demurred. He wanted an Internet-based system. The CIO disagreed. Technology was the CIO's strong suit, but he was in no way ignorant of VSI's key business drivers. He understood that regulatory requirements (and basic decency) obligated the firm to protect the privacy of patient information, and guaranteeing privacy on the Internet was difficult. Further, the firm's business model demanded 100 percent uptime for its systems, and that was difficult to promise on the Internet. The company's virtual workers couldn't produce transcripts when the system was down, so a less-than-bulletproof system would jeopardize the transcription turnaround times promised customers.

Despite the CIO's strong case that the Internet could guarantee neither availability (uptime) nor access control (privacy), the CFO insisted on an Internet-based solution. After several rounds of mutually unsatisfying discussions, the management team realized what the two executives were really arguing about. It was risk—specifically, the different tolerances of the CIO and CFO for specific risk trade-offs. Although the CIO believed the company and its customers had zero tolerance for process outages (availability risks) and privacy violations (access risks), the CFO was most concerned about threats to agility. Two strategies in particular—making the firm easier for clients to work with, and hiring offshore as well as onshore transcriptionists—were essential to the senior team's plans, and as the CFO saw it, the Internet was key to both.

Once the senior team realized that the argument was not about technology but about which IT risks were most important to the firm, members saw that the technical decision was really a business decision, and they quickly came to consensus. Reducing agility risk came first, with access and availability risk a close second. All parties agreed that an Internet-based approach addressed agility risk better than the CIO's proprietary approach. "Good enough" reduction for access and availability risks could be achieved by adding protections like encryption and redundancy to an Internet-based system; that came at a higher cost, but it was well below the savings that would be achieved by easy access to offshore labor. With the most important risks managed to an acceptable level, the team moved forward immediately and rapidly implemented the new system.

In this first chapter, we have described the importance of viewing IT risk as the potential for an unplanned event involving IT to threaten any of four critical enterprise objectives: availability, access, accuracy, and agility. We've discussed the ways in which this framework—the 4A's—changes the nature of the discussion between IT and business personnel. The 4A's make it possible to discuss IT risk in terms of business consequences and thus help executives get comfortable doing what they are good at—making decisions in the face of business risks—for IT risks.

But this is only the first step. Making trade-offs among the four risks, and being clear about the enterprise's relative tolerance to each one, just sets direction. The next step is to build the organizational capability that shapes and maintains the enterprise risk profile. In the next chapter, we'll discuss the most important tools for building a successful IT risk management capability: the three core disciplines of IT risk management.

Two

The Three Core Disciplines of IT Risk Management

IMAGINE THAT you're the CEO (or CFO or CIO) of a large U.S. financial services company. For twenty years, the firm has grown rapidly through acquisitions and through the entrepreneurial actions of its seven autonomous business units. Now things are changing. Because growth is slowing, your team is shifting strategy from product-line growth to cross-selling, up-selling, and globalizing. Customers and business partners are starting to demand an integrated approach—asking your fiercely independent business units to look and act like a unified team. Worse, auditors are becoming a problem: your external auditors are paying more attention to IT, your regulators have begun IT-specific audits, and your business partners' auditors are now auditing you, too.

These strategic issues are linked closely to IT risks. You are sure some of the business units (but not all) have nagging availability and access risks that they are not telling you about. Accuracy risk, which is under control within each business unit (or so you're told), is a significant problem now that customers and regulators are demanding accurate enterprisewide information. For example, it was difficult to certify financial reports for Sarbanes-Oxley, and accurate, up-to-date reporting of all activity with individual clients is more than a year away. Furthermore, you're having trouble convincing the top managers that they need to change the way they invest and work with IT. After all, each business unit president feels he gets enough agility from his dedicated IT staff and doesn't want to threaten his own unit's results to improve enterprise IT agility.

These are just the IT risks you can guess. There are surely more that you should know about but don't. You know you need to do something about IT risk—fast. But where do you start? Do you bring in a consulting firm to rewrite systems? Implement a strong management process to identify and fix every risk? Educate your business unit colleagues on the importance of IT risk and hope they'll change their own organizations?

Our research has defined a straightforward approach that answers these questions. In the simplest terms, IT risk management capability is built on three core disciplines. The three core disciplines work together as a cohesive whole to improve the enterprise's risk profile and keep it under control. They are:

- A well-structured *foundation* of IT assets—an installed technology base of infrastructure and application technologies, and supporting personnel and procedures, that is well understood, well managed, and no more complex than absolutely necessary

- A well-designed and executed *risk governance process* that provides an enterprise-level view of all risks, so that executives can prioritize and invest appropriately in risk management, while enabling lower-level managers to independently manage most risks in their areas

- A *risk-aware culture* in which everyone has appropriate knowledge of risk and in which open, nonthreatening discussions of risk are the norm[1]

An enterprise that wants to make the most effective use of its scarce resources in managing IT risks must be competent in all three. But in any particular enterprise, some disciplines are an easier sell than others. Accordingly, many risk managers choose a focal discipline as a rallying point for risk management, using it to make the case for change and to improve all three disciplines over time. The choice of focal discipline depends on the enterprise's circumstances— including factors such as size, industry, and capabilities—and our research shows that successful IT risk management initiatives can begin with any of the three disciplines.

The three disciplines complement the 4A's. Discussing the 4A's sets a direction for the firm's IT risk management capability by specifying a desired risk profile and appropriate risk trade-offs. The three disciplines implement capabilities that shape the IT risk profile to match the enterprise's preferences on the 4A's. Then, closing the loop, the three disciplines provide information for further discussion and decision making at all levels of the enterprise.

Building the three disciplines does more than help the enterprise manage IT risks better. It also gives executives something that is all too often a luxury in a world of ever-increasing IT threats: confidence. You gain confidence that you know what your most important risks are, that you have an effective process to make decisions about those risks, and that managers throughout the organization have the ability to handle those risks effectively. In our study, firms that were more confident in their IT risk management capabilities reported more control over all four IT risks, were significantly less

FIGURE 2-1

The core disciplines of risk management

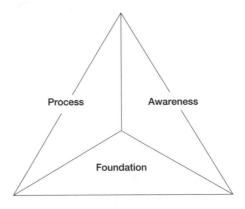

Source: © 2007 MIT Sloan Center for Information Systems Research and Gartner. Adapted from George Westerman, "Building IT Risk Management Effectiveness," Research Briefing IV(2C) (Cambridge, MA: Center for Information Systems Research, July 2004). Used with permission.

likely to say they were unaware of important IT risks, and enjoyed significantly better relationships between the IT organization and business executives—all while spending only a fraction more than other firms on IT risk management.

Figure 2-1 depicts the three disciplines as a triangle composed of three equal segments. The disciplines are complementary; each addresses different aspects of the 4A's by improving organization, technology, procedures, and behaviors. Together, they cover all the bases—improving risk management capability and giving business and IT people a language to ensure that IT risks stay under control.

Let's look at each of the three disciplines in more detail.

The Foundation

The foundation discipline addresses the 4A's in terms of technology and procedure by strengthening the *foundation*: that is, the collection of IT assets, procedures, and people that support and enable business processes and decision making. This includes:

- Infrastructure that supports a wide range of computing, information management, and communications activities throughout the enterprise (this includes common technologies such as networks and computers, nonbusiness-process-specific applications such as e-mail and word processors, and common support functions such as an IT help desk)

- Applications that support the tasks and processes of the business, such as financial reporting systems, supply chain systems, and even the spreadsheets and decision support systems used by planners

- People with the skills to manage the foundation

- Processes and mechanisms for monitoring, control, and maintenance to keep these assets running smoothly and safely

As we said earlier, a solid IT foundation is well understood, well managed, and no more complex than absolutely necessary. A house built on a poor foundation suffers creaks, shakes, sagging, and eventual collapse. Owners must use heroic methods to prop up sagging floors and fix leaky plumbing caused by the structure's shifting over time. Organizations built on a shaky IT foundation are no different. Their owners are constantly propping up weaknesses and fixing leaks instead of enjoying the benefits of a well-built structure.

A solid IT foundation is risk resistant in many ways:

- *Problems are less likely.* Cracks and holes in the foundation are fixed through solid management processes. Intermittent and hidden bugs that are so common in complex systems are much less likely to be present.

- *When problems and failures happen, they are more quickly and easily diagnosed and repaired.* Lower complexity makes the causes of problems more apparent, and technical personnel are much more likely to understand what has gone wrong and how to fix the issue.

- *It is easier to assess risks.* The number of variables that bear on risk, such as the frailties and limitations of specific technologies or the detailed knowledge of specific configurations, is smaller. Monitoring and control processes are more easily configured to detect risky conditions.

- *It is easier to maintain.* Standardization allows technicians to make patches (i.e., fixes to things that weren't supposed to break to begin with) and upgrades using the same parts and procedures for all components, rather than having to understand different procedures for each component.

- *It is easier to change.* In a complex foundation, IT people must often change many components in many different places and then do extensive, complex testing to make sure all the changes work together. In a simplified foundation, change requires tinkering in fewer places, and testing can be done in a very straightforward way.

In short, a solid foundation avoids the opacity, complexity, frailty, and inattention that breed IT risk in most large organizations.

A Weak Foundation Amplifies All Risks

A weak foundation obviously creates risks related to availability and access. But the risks often go much further, impacting the company and its customers through threats to accuracy and agility. For example, one major insurance company's systems could not provide accurate, complete, and up-to-date information on policies and claims, which complicated customer service. An internal study showed that the revenue loss from canceled policies was equivalent to the entire revenue from new premiums each year, and an incident involving poor customer service was the precipitating factor in over 80 percent of policy cancellations. The threat to long-term profitability was even greater, given that the typical insurance sales commission structure makes a policy unprofitable until it is several years old. Essentially, accuracy risks caused by a weak foundation and the resulting customer service problems forced the company to trade profitable current business for unprofitable new business—in effect, making it run faster and faster just to fall further and further behind. The study prompted executives to undertake a major transformation of the firm's IT foundation, not only as a risk control strategy, but as a growth strategy.

Fixing the Foundation Is a Journey

The first and most basic step to improving the foundation discipline is to examine the foundation and implement basic controls to ensure that there are no major weaknesses waiting to become catastrophes and to implement processes for recovery in the event of failure. The next step is to reduce complexity in infrastructure and applications, ultimately the most cost-effective way to reduce risk in the organization for the long term.

It is important to understand the terms *infrastructure* and *applications*: IT infrastructure is the platform that enables business applications to operate reliably; it consists of technical platforms (e.g., processing power, storage, networking, database, and middleware), people, nonbusiness-process-specific software such as e-mail or spreadsheets, and supporting services such as the help desk. Applications are the business-process-specific software that runs on the infrastructure.[2]

Although simplifying the foundation's infrastructure and applications requires up-front investment, which may be substantial, more substantial cost savings follow rapidly. In many cases significant initial steps toward simplification can be accomplished without dramatically affecting business processes. This means that the impact of change on the enterprise can be minimized while risks *and* costs are reduced.

Almost any enterprise can succeed in simplifying its technology infrastructure, and the financial case alone is compelling, as we describe in our detailed discussion of the foundation discipline in chapters 3 and 4. But simplifying applications is much more costly, difficult, and disruptive to the entire organization. Therefore, making foundation simplification the centerpiece of IT risk management is usually feasible only when the business is able to build (or rebuild) its entire foundation of infrastructure and applications from scratch. This is, of course, what start-ups do, but relatively few established companies with inventories of existing legacy applications—aging, risky technologies whose continuing value to the business makes them difficult to abandon—are willing or able to do so. (The CIO of one government agency defined a *legacy system* for us as follows: "It's a system that's a hindrance in some way, but it's delivering business value, so you can't just get rid of it.")

When firms cannot start from a green field, they often choose a more gradual approach, changing the IT foundation chunk by chunk, beginning with infrastructure, and using each new business initiative to simplify a part of the applications. In this way, they gradually simplify, standardize, and strengthen the foundation.

In summary, the foundation discipline is the most cost-effective way to reduce IT risk. Immediately implementing controls and recovery processes reduces the likelihood and impact of risk in the current foundation. Simplification reduces both risk and ongoing maintenance and support costs. But in an enterprise with a substantial preexisting inventory of IT assets, the foundation discipline is the most difficult, time-consuming, and resource-intensive of the three disciplines. After the initial effort to bring the foundation to acceptable levels, firms with a large, complex inventory of applications typically choose to make either governance process or awareness, not foundation, their main focus. (For an overview of this discipline, see "A Summary of the Foundation Discipline.")

A Summary of the Foundation Discipline

The foundation is the collection of IT assets, procedures, and people that support and enable business processes and decision making. Bringing the foundation to a competent level—knowing what is in the foundation and ensuring that it is managed well—is essential for all enterprises. Many enterprises then work to make the foundation excellent by ensuring that it is only as complex as absolutely necessary.

Benefits of a foundation-driven approach:

- Immediately finding and fixing holes in the foundation corrects immediate weaknesses, providing time to make other longer-term improvements.

- Simplification is the most cost-effective risk management approach over the long term because it pays off in cost reduction as well as risk reduction.

- Simplification reduces all four IT risks and makes the other two disciplines easier to master.

Issues with a foundation-driven approach:

- Initial efforts to find and fix holes can be substantial.

- It can be difficult and costly to go beyond simplifying the infrastructure to simplify the applications.

- Simplification takes time. It is most often done incrementally.

We discuss the foundation discipline in detail in chapters 3 and 4.

The Risk Governance Process

The discipline of IT risk governance process addresses the 4A's organizationally and procedurally, ensuring that the organization has the necessary structures and processes to systematically identify and manage risks. This discipline creates and manages the processes, procedures, and organizational structures needed to:

- Define and maintain policy and standards

- Identify and prioritize risks

- Manage risks and monitor risk trends over time

- Ensure compliance with risk policy and standards

The risk governance process is the force that pulls otherwise fragmented, localized views of IT risk together into a comprehensive whole, allowing the enterprise to effectively set priorities and act. No centralized person or group has a wide enough perspective to fully understand and control all risks in even a moderate-sized organization. Local managers are best positioned to understand and manage risks in different parts of the organization. But even if those managers are aware of risk and engaged in managing it, their perspective is incomplete, and their priorities may differ from the enterprise as a whole. The organization needs mechanisms for local managers to identify and resolve risks *and* a consolidated view of risk that enables it to prioritize, invest in solutions, and monitor results at the enterprise level. The risk governance process is the means to both.

Most large enterprises lead their IT risk management with an effective risk governance process. For all enterprises, it is essential to be competent at this discipline as rapidly as possible.

When an enterprise's IT risk governance discipline is weak, the business has a fragmented, spotty view of risk. Some business units identify and handle risks much better than others. Audits are a recurring nightmare. Surprises are frequent. In the words of one CIO we interviewed, "I realized my biggest risk was that I didn't know what my IT risks were."

The fragmented view of risk that results from weak risk governance process carries significant dangers:

- *The full extent of a given risk and its priority compared to other risks are not understood.* Failure to address the most important risks first leads to dangerous exposures. Nearly all managers believe that their risks are the most important in the enterprise (or at least they say so)—but whose risks really matter most? Is a threat to availability in financial systems as important as the same risk in factory systems? How about the access, accuracy, and availability risks of computer virus attacks versus the agility risk of extending the integration period of a merger? Unless the enterprise has a process to examine and compare all IT risks, it can easily be distracted by the most visible and apparently urgent risk, whether or not that risk is the most important.

- *Spending and resources devoted to risk are not well understood.* Fragmentation hides the level of spending as well as the extent of risk. Our data shows that CIOs tend to seriously underestimate—by 100–200 percent on average—the amount of resources they devote to risk management. The most important reason for this miscalculation, we believe, is that the spending on risk management is compartmentalized—managed in multiple departments, by multiple managers, in multiple budgets.

- *The effectiveness of risk management efforts is not understood.* When risk oversight is fragmented, it's difficult to know whether efforts are producing the desired results and where, how, and why they are succeeding or failing. Many of the people we surveyed for our study were concerned that they didn't know whether they were spending too much or too little on risk management; others were concerned that they weren't spending on the right things. Effective risk governance process eliminates much of that uncertainty.

- *Some risks are bigger than a single person or business unit.* When a person encounters an overwhelming risk and no help or support is available, his usual reaction is to push the risk to the back of his mind and try not to worry about it. (This, in a nutshell, is why life insurance, as the industry's conventional wisdom has it, is sold and not bought.) A risk governance process that manages risks up, down, and across the enterprise chain of command helps protect individual managers from risks whose impacts and solutions are beyond their personal scope of control—and from giving up and hoping that luck will solve the problem.

Finding the right type and balance of autonomy and control in a risk governance process takes experimentation in every enterprise. The right pace is important. In some enterprises risk governance benefits by starting loose and becoming tighter, while other enterprises may use tight risk governance to gain attention and rapidly reduce risks, easing the rigorous governance as awareness grows. All three risk management disciplines require resources, but the resources devoted to a risk governance process seem particularly onerous to many enterprises—especially those that demand provable ROI from every initiative. (As the global vice president of IT risk management in one major pharmaceutical company told us, "You can't prove that something never happened because of your IT risk management program.") Organizations that are historically immature in their processes or that are culturally hostile to visitors from headquarters who offer help may reject governance of any sort. Especially in smaller businesses, the overhead associated with a risk governance process seems like a lot of trouble and expense. That said, a risk governance process tailored to enterprise needs is essential, since it is the only way to have a full view of the risks facing the enterprise.

For an overview of this discipline, see "A Summary of the Risk Governance Process Discipline." We discuss the risk governance process and considerations for its implementation in detail in chapter 5.

A Summary of the Risk Governance Process Discipline

Risk governance is the set of processes, policies, and structures that provide an enterprise-level view of all risks, so that executives can prioritize and invest appropriately in risk management, while it enables lower-level managers to independently manage most risks in their areas.

Benefits of a risk-governance-driven approach:

- It ensures an enterprisewide view of IT risk.
- It is best for integrating risk management with strategy.
- It highlights areas that are under- or overinvesting in risk. Issues with a risk-governance-driven approach:
- There is potentially high overhead.
- If risk governance process is poorly managed, it can introduce bottlenecks and delays.
- It may be seen as just another administrative hurdle to jump (or avoid).

We discuss the risk governance discipline in detail in chapter 5.

A Risk-Aware Culture

The discipline of risk awareness addresses the 4A's in terms of personal responsibility and behavior. A risk-aware culture is one that has:

- Deep *expertise* in particular aspects of IT risk, which is typically held and used by specialists

- *Generalized awareness* throughout the enterprise of the nature and consequences of risky behavior and how to avoid them

- A *culture* that explicitly encourages everyone, at every level of the enterprise, to discuss risk openly and take personal responsibility for managing it

Regardless of how well structured its foundation is, no enterprise can manage risk well unless it has people who are aware of risk and willing to do something about it. Without deep expertise, basic technical and procedural protections can't be effectively implemented and managed. Without general awareness, people throughout the enterprise make easily preventable mistakes with serious consequences. Without a culture that encourages open discussion of risk and a shared responsibility for managing it, risky conditions are hidden from sight, or managers buffer themselves from risk with every means at their disposal.

Technology Only Goes So Far in Reducing Risk

At chemical company Hoechst/Celanese, whose case we discuss in detail in chapter 6, a risk-averse culture led project managers to ask for (and receive) far more money and time than they thought they would need as protection against unforeseen risks.[3] The managers always hit their targets. But their risk-averse culture increased risk to agility. The firm could not handle any but the most simple challenges quickly, a problem that became a survival issue when major challenges appeared in the wake of a management buyout. The new management, in addition to improving the IT foundation, also undertook the challenge of changing the risk-averse culture to a risk-aware one.

Having good risk awareness is *not* about being risk averse. It's about being cognizant of risks and making smart decisions about them. Enterprises with a risk-aware culture take on more risks, but they're not more risky. They're just smarter about which risks they will take and how they will manage those risks.

Risk Awareness Is Built from the Top Down

A risk-aware culture demands that people sometimes prioritize enterprise risks above their own, that people share information about their risks and help others resolve their risks (often without personal gain), and that they sometimes take big, visible risks that have a chance of failure. This is not normal behavior in most large organizations, where incentives, policies, and politics generally favor risk aversion over smart risk awareness.

Only active engagement and support from the top of the enterprise can produce this kind of behavior. Executives in a risk-aware culture show—through their actions, investments, and behaviors—that risk management and the acceptance of calculated risk are part of the way the enterprise does business. This is not easy. It takes determination and focus to ask about the risks inherent in every new business initiative, to follow risk-related policies and governance rules even when it's difficult or inconvenient, to make risk an acceptable subject for conversation and occasional failure an acceptable (if not desirable) outcome.

Awareness is often the discipline of choice for smaller, agile enterprises, where the culture is already conducive to taking risks, sharing information, and helping each other. Even when large firms start with awareness (like EquipCo, whose story we tell in chapter 7), they typically transition to a risk-governance-driven approach over time. For an overview of this discipline, see "A Summary of the Risk Awareness Discipline." We discuss the awareness discipline in more detail in chapter 6.

Every enterprise needs all three disciplines. A well-structured, well-managed IT foundation is inherently less risky than a more complex one. A risk-aware culture helps people recognize and deal openly with threats, risky behaviors, and risk reduction opportunities. And a mature risk governance process systematically develops a comprehensive picture of enterprise risks, bringing the full resources of the business to bear on risks that exceed the resources and authority of any single manager.

A Summary of the Risk Awareness Discipline

The risk awareness discipline builds an enterprise in which everyone, at every level, is aware of risk, discusses risk, and takes a personal responsibility for managing it. Risk-aware firms are characterized by a deep expertise in particular aspects of IT risk, which is typically held and used by specialists. They also build a generalized awareness throughout the enterprise of the nature and consequences of risky behavior, and encourage a culture in which risk is discussed and managed openly.

Benefits of an awareness-driven approach:

- Awareness is essential; even the best process can fail if it is built around uninformed people.

All three disciplines are necessary, but few enterprises give equal emphasis to all of them. Once dangerous conditions in the foundation are fixed, an enterprise can focus on the discipline that makes the most sense for the business. With that discipline as the driver, all three can be evolved into a stable, cohesive, comprehensive capability that systematically addresses the business trade-offs implicit in the 4A's.

Our research shows that most firms make either awareness or risk governance the focus of their programs, though there are good reasons to tackle the foundation first, as we describe in the next chapter. Whatever the focus, the goal is to embed risk management into the fabric of the enterprise. Effective risk management is achieved when risk management is part of the way that the enterprise does business—procedurally, technologically, organizationally, and behaviorally.

- Focused expertise helps the whole organization understand and resolve risks.
- Risk-aware culture improves willingness to discuss and manage risks as a team, rather than requiring individuals to fully manage their own risks.

Issues with an awareness-driven approach:

- It requires the visible attention of and role modeling from top executives; without their public support, effectiveness is limited.
- Awareness cannot be built by training alone; it must be incorporated into policy, processes, and culture.
- Companies can fail to achieve a balance between expertise and general awareness.

We discuss the risk awareness discipline in detail in chapter 6.

Three

Fixing the Foundation

Strengthening the Base of the Pyramid

E XECUTIVES OF semiconductor manufacturer ChipCo enjoy a real-time view of order status and inventory levels and a single integrated view of financials, orders, and manufacturing around the globe.[1] The company can do a quarterly financial close in as little as two days. Customers can see the status of their orders in real time on a secure Web site. The supply chain vice president can shift production flexibly across fabrication sites as needed.

Few enterprises can match these capabilities. But most enterprises, unlike ChipCo, do not build their core business processes on a simplified, standardized base of infrastructure and applications. By structuring its IT foundation to be as simple as possible from the start, ChipCo has reaped business value while driving out cost and IT risk.

Twelve years ago, when ChipCo was only one-fourth its current size, the CIO and his team implemented a single enterprisewide ERP package. They built a secure, reliable, standardized infrastructure to host it and supported the infrastructure with knowledgeable IT staff. They integrated the package with ChipCo's standard manufacturing systems at each fabrication site, or "fab." Over the past ten years, as the company quadrupled in size, this focus on simplified, standardized technologies kept IT costs in check even as the IT team delivered a range of high-quality services, including a secure customer Web site and an integrated global supply chain.

ChipCo's low-risk IT foundation includes:

- A standardized infrastructure for processing and communications worldwide

- A single global ERP presence linked to a set of standard manufacturing systems in the fabs (other applications— including e-business—are well integrated into the global ERP backbone)

- Global access to designs (subject to access controls) for engineers in any of the firm's design offices

- IT staff who know the systems and how those systems support the business processes

- Business continuity management that is updated and tested often

- Controls to keep the security perimeter protected and to limit unauthorized access inside the perimeter

- Controls to ensure that the foundation is safe and that unnecessary complexity and risk do not enter the foundation

ChipCo's tight management of its foundation reduces risks to all 4A's. Availability and access risks are reduced because the foundation is well designed and only as complex as necessary. Accuracy risks are low because the single worldwide system removes potential conflicts and redundancies in the base data. And agility risk is low because, for the kinds of agility ChipCo needs (launching new products, enhancing customer services, and changing the product mix, not engaging in major mergers and acquisitions or unrelated diversification), the well-structured foundation can be easily extended.

Most enterprises do not have the advantage of an IT foundation that was built for low risk from the start. Often IT foundations are full of complexity: many different types of hardware, many applications integrated in unpredictable ways (if at all), technology so old that few people understand what's inside it anymore. These kinds of conditions, the legacy of years of IT management focused on fulfilling particular business requests but not governing with an overall eye toward risk, create risk for the enterprise. For most firms, shoring up the foundation is a long and complex challenge—but ultimately rewarding in terms of financial returns, business performance, and low IT risk. (To learn about what makes a foundation effective, see "What Is a Solid Foundation?")

Fix the Foundation—It Pays

Our survey research shows that firms with a well-managed, simplified foundation have statistically significantly lower IT risk in *all* 4A's. What's more, fixing the foundation offers immediate financial benefits even while it reduces risk. By improving the firm's operations, structure, and staff knowledge of infrastructure and applications, fixing the foundation produces an IT environment that is less costly, less complex, more robust, and less prone to error or failure.

How much less costly? The typical IT organization spends 20–50 percent (sometimes as much as 70 percent) of its budget on infrastructure alone.[2] Simplification reliably reduces that figure by 10–35 percent, or anywhere from 2 percent to more than 17 percent of the overall IT budget.[3] DuPont's infrastructure simplification program,

What Is a Solid IT Foundation?

A solid, low-risk IT foundation is a cleanly structured set of technologies and applications that is well managed and has sufficient controls and support in place to keep it strong. It has the following properties:

- Standardized infrastructure, which uses only the necessary required number of different technology configurations and no more

- A well-integrated base of applications that is only as complex as absolutely necessary

- Documented data structures and process definitions that are consistent throughout the enterprise

- Controlled access to data and applications, with built-in mechanisms to prevent unauthorized actions and detect anomalies

- Support staff who know what is in each application and how each technology supports each business process

- Maintenance processes that keep technology up-to-date with required security patches and upgrades and that provide adequate protection in the event of a technology failure

---

under way but not yet completed, has already reduced its ongoing IT operations costs by tens of millions of dollars *per year*.[4] Novartis was able to save more than $225 million over four years by consolidating and standardizing infrastructure, with little or no disruption to the business.[5]

To put it bluntly, given the financial, operational, and risk reduction payoffs, few enterprises can afford *not* to simplify the foundation. How can an enterprise fix a complex, creaky foundation without completely disrupting business? The answer is to fix things in the right order—the order that offers the most leverage for investments in resources, staffing, and managerial attention. That order is from the bottom to the top of the IT risk pyramid.

Start at the Base of the IT Risk Pyramid and Move Up

Our analysis of the survey data shows that risk factors related to availability, access, accuracy, and agility form a hierarchy, which we call the "IT risk pyramid" (see figure 3-1).[6]

FIGURE 3-1

The IT risk pyramid

Analysis of 134 surveys shows that risk factors for a given enterprise IT risk (level of the pyramid) are statistically significantly correlated with the amount of not only that risk but also one or more risks above it in the pyramid.

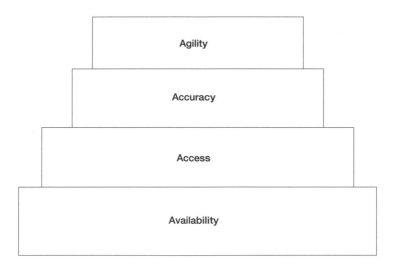

Source: © 2007 MIT Sloan Center for Information Systems Research. Adapted from George Westerman, "The IT Risk Pyramid: Where to Start with Risk Management," Research Briefing V(1D) (Cambridge, MA: Center for Information Systems Research, March 2005). Used with permission.

The importance of the pyramid is that each factor in a given tier influences not only risks in that tier but also risks in tiers above it. For example, the availability risk factor of complex, nonstandardized infrastructure affects everything in the pyramid hierarchy, from the bottom up:

- *Availability* risk increases because having many different types of technology makes it harder to ensure that all technology assets are properly maintained and that the enterprise has the tools and skills to fix whatever might fail.

- *Access* risk increases because it is difficult to manage access controls across a multitude of platforms that are integrated in unclear ways or to ensure that all the different configurations stay up-to-date with software patches.

- *Accuracy* risk increases because of the difficulty of manually integrating information across disparate systems. Even writing automatic integration links can be difficult when connecting diverse technologies or translating between different definitions and versions of essentially the same information. For example, consolidating across two systems that recognize a "sale" differently can be very complex, if not impossible.

- Finally, *agility* risk increases. Systems are difficult to extend or convert, and it is hard to understand how a change in one might impact others. Any business change requires investigating and changing multiple systems, followed by extensive testing and reworking to address unexpected problems. The result is constraints on business models and strategic choices.

Figure 3-2 shows key IT risk factors aligned with their tiers in the pyramid.

FIGURE 3-2

Key IT risk factors and the IT risk pyramid

Analysis of 134 surveys shows that risk factors for a given enterprise IT risk (level of the pyramid) are statistically significantly correlated with the amount of not only that risk, but also one or more risks above it in the pyramid.

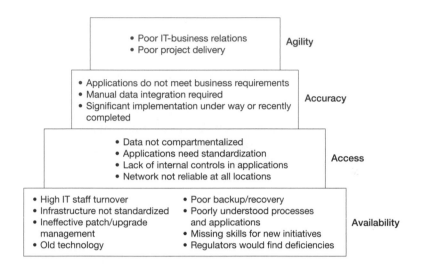

Source: © 2007 MIT Sloan Center for Information Systems Research. Adapted from George Westerman, "The IT Risk Pyramid: Where to Start with Risk Management," Research Briefing V(1D) (Cambridge, MA: Center for Information Systems Research, March 2005). Used with permission.

Addressing risk tiers from bottom to top is the highest-leverage approach to IT risk reduction. It is also the easiest path in terms of organizational impact. In every respect, the organizational issues associated with IT risk management are easier to manage at the base of the risk pyramid:

- It is easier to justify ROI for risk reductions in lower tiers, where the risks are all on the more easily quantifiable downside, than it is for those in higher tiers, where risks are on the less quantifiable upside.

- Hard-dollar payoffs at the bottom happen immediately; payoffs at the top may take years.

- The organizational risks and difficulties involved in change itself are much greater at the top of the pyramid than at the bottom. Change at the top involves a larger cross-section of the enterprise and reaches deeper into business processes.

- The IT organization has near-total control over risk factors at the bottom, making decisions and resolutions simpler and more focused, but reducing risks at the top involves risk factors that are well beyond the IT organization's reach.

- Higher-tier risks can't be fully resolved until the base of the pyramid is under control. Stopgap solutions often must be reworked later to reduce complexity and improve accuracy or agility.

In addition to being the highest-leverage approach to IT risk reduction, addressing risk factors and tiers from bottom to top is the most organizationally and politically feasible. In short, if you want to renovate your house, fix the big cracks in the foundation first.

Follow the Three-Step Process to Fixing the Base

In the remainder of this chapter, we describe a program for bringing the base of the pyramid up to a competent level. This includes three steps:

1. First, address availability risks by managing business continuity to ensure that the organization can get up and running again quickly if a major incident occurs.

2. Concurrently, identify and plug holes in the foundation, using IT audit and the knowledge of the IT team as a guide, to address availability and access risks.

3. Then implement basic IT controls and industry best prac
tices to monitor the status of the base and prevent future
holes in the foundation.

After your organization completes those three steps, you can
start the longer-term work of simplifying the foundation, as we will
describe in chapter 4. Of course, each of these steps is worthy of a
book-length treatment, which is well beyond the scope of this discussion. We look at each element of the improvement process briefly
in this chapter. Experts in each of these areas are plentiful and ready
to help with detailed implementations.

Build and Test a Business Continuity Plan

Business continuity management (BCM) is about understanding and
reducing the potential for catastrophic events to impact critical business processes. It is a fundamental part of availability risk management—the base of the IT risk pyramid. Other steps to improving the
foundation reduce the likelihood of availability problems, but BCM
is about managing the impact of dangerous events, however unlikely they may be.

BCM is a powerful engine that pulls a remarkably long train. It
exposes important weaknesses and risks in the base of the IT risk pyramid, it mitigates some of the most immediately serious risks the enterprise will ever face, and it lays the groundwork for long-term risk management in every tier of the IT risk pyramid, improving management of
all 4A's. Furthermore, it changes the way business and IT people work
together to manage crisis, it helps IT people understand the trade-offs
and business consequences of IT risk, and it helps executives understand the business value supported by IT and their role in ensuring
that value is realized. Finally, BCM creates important benefits beyond
crisis recovery. A striking example is Wal-Mart and Home Depot's

readiness after Hurricane Katrina in 2006, which produced enormous benefits, including exceptional goodwill and loyalty, for the companies, their employees and other stakeholders, and their communities.[7]

Many enterprises have not yet installed effective BCM. As of mid-2005, only 25 percent of the *Fortune* 2000 had an enterprisewide business continuity plan, and less than 50 percent of the *Fortune* 2000 had tested their disaster recovery plans—a more limited plan for recovering IT systems only—within the preceding twelve months.[8] When disaster strikes, most enterprises are inadequately prepared. And the incidents described in the introduction should leave no doubt that disaster strikes more often than any business likes and whether or not it is ready.

Most enterprises spend about 2 percent of their IT budget—or six-tenths of one percent of revenue, on average—on BCM.[9] As a

Key Steps to Effective Business Continuity Management

1. Understand IT assets and availability risks.

   - Conduct a business impact analysis, and use it to prioritize spending on the most critical business processes.

   - Develop an inventory of IT and business assets, and link the inventory to business processes.

2. Create a plan.

   - Build an incident management plan, team, and process. Document preferred communication channels and methods in the incident response plan.

   - Establish a service-level classification and testing scheme (e.g., gold-, silver-, and bronze-level service) for availability and business continuity.

rough rule of thumb, if the enterprise does not have an up-to-date enterprisewide business continuity plan or the plan has not been successfully tested in the past twelve months, then more attention and resources should be devoted to BCM. We emphasize that attention, especially from business executives, is what matters most. IT personnel will do their best to identify which business processes and supporting IT systems are the highest priorities for recovery, but without business help, they may not be correct. Additionally, IT personnel manage only technology resources, which are far from all the resources that are necessary to recover a business process.

The box "Key Steps to Effective Business Continuity Management" describes how to build an effective BCM program. The sections that follow provide further detail.

- Develop contingency plans for expanded scenarios, such as regional events, and plans to mitigate the risks of external events.

3. Implement and test the plan.

- Build business continuity into the business and IT project life cycles to ensure recovery of people, technology, facilities, and business processes.

- Define standard and repeatable development, infrastructure, and operations architectures to meet the required service levels.

- Create an employee notification system for large events, and train employees.

- Test at least annually. If comprehensive testing is not practical, perform walk-through testing, and ensure that external dependencies are addressed.

Source: Gartner, Inc. research.

Use Business Impact Analysis to Set Priorities and Timelines for Recovery

The most effective way to prioritize low-likelihood events, such as process outages, is to compare the impact of each potential incident. Accordingly, the first step in BCM is performing a business impact analysis (BIA). The BIA takes senior management's discussion of tolerance for availability risk (as described in chapter 1) to a detailed level, including assessment of how failure in specific business processes will affect the business over time, hour by hour and day by day, and the circumstances in which processes might fail.

One division of a medium-sized financial services company discovered, in its first BIA, that failure in one of its customer service processes would cost $6 million in the first twenty-four hours—and if recovery was not complete by the end of the first week, the division would be out of business. (Losses on that scale are minor for many companies; for a credit card service provider in Brazil that we interviewed, losses in the millions of dollars occurred within the first *thirty minutes* of a point-of-sale network outage.) BIA can identify the highest-impact processes so that they can get priority attention.

After performing a BIA, mapping technology and business assets to business processes creates an inventory list of facilities and equipment that must be recovered or replaced when the business process fails. The technology inventory helps IT managers prioritize equipment, applications, and networks, but this is not the only part of the recovery problem. Business assets are often more difficult, time consuming, and expensive to acquire in a catastrophe than replacement computer equipment. A Gartner study of New York City enterprises that were directly involved in the 9/11 attacks found that the majority recovered their computing assets quickly but that procuring office space was a recurring problem. The World Trade Center towers and nearby buildings contained office space equal to the entire inventory of Atlanta, and some businesses had to move several times before they found permanent quarters.[10]

Create a Plan

The BIA helps prioritize the recovery of each business process in the event of failure. If all else is equal (including process dependencies, the extent of damage, and other factors), highest-impact processes should be recovered first. To ease the prioritization process—especially in scenarios that involve simultaneous failure of multiple processes, such as the destruction or unavailability of an entire campus—many enterprises classify processes with similar impact into groups. Table 3-1 shows a classification scheme, developed by Gartner researchers Roberta Witty and Tom Wagner, that describes required service levels for different kinds of applications, based on business purpose and criticality. Applying standardized processes and timelines for recovery to each class ensures that resources go where they're needed first in a crisis.

TABLE 3-1

Example of service classification levels

	Business	Service level	Recommendations
Class 1	Customer- or partner-facing	• 24 × 7 scheduled • 99.9%	Yearly "war gaming" (unannounced full-scale simulated disaster or attack scenario) Full tests every six months after
Class 2	Less critical revenue-producing	• 24 × 6 + 18 hours (6 hours reserved for maintenance window) • 99.5%	"Desktop" tests every six months and full yearly tests after
Class 3	Company back-office functions	• 18 × 7 scheduled • 99%	"Desktop" tests every six months and full yearly tests after
Class 4	Departmental functions	• 24 × 6 + 12 hours (12 hours reserved for maintenance window) • 98%	"Desktop" tests every six months and full yearly tests after

Source: © 2006 Gartner, Inc. Adapted from Roberta Witty and Tom Wagner, "Business Continuity Management Today: From Hurricanes to Blackouts to Terrorism," paper presented at Gartner IT Security Summit, June 5–7, 2006.

BIA and service classifications clarify the sequence of recovery but not the actual recovery process. Each business process needs an incident management plan that clearly defines the process of recovery, including the responsibilities, conditions, and mechanisms for initiating an incident response; assembling the team, performing an initial assessment of the situation; escalating notification and oversight to higher levels in the company; managing communications and incident resolution; and officially closing the book on an incident.

Regional catastrophes are relatively rare, but when they occur, an enterprise can find itself competing for scarce resources with every other business in its region. Most enterprises establish their backup data centers far enough from the primary center to be insulated from a single catastrophic incident. But very well-prepared enterprises go a step further and make plans for the essential infrastructure—including transportation, supplies, communications, and power—that they will need in the wake of a regional disaster until they can relocate outside the disaster zone.

Smaller enterprises, in particular, may lack the resources to compensate for the loss of basic services in a regional disaster.[11] An insurance company in the southern United States has good reason to invest in disaster recovery: its region is frequently hit by hurricanes, and it cannot relocate away from its main customer base. But other enterprises may find it difficult to make the business case for a full-scale disaster recovery capability in less disaster-prone areas. Regardless of scale, some preparation in this regard is much better than none. Most BCM incidents are not regional disasters; but planning for these smaller events is just as important, and the practice gained with them will still be useful if a larger-scale disaster does happen. In the wake of the 9/11 attacks, businesses that had created and practiced business continuity plans succeeded in recovering operations fairly quickly, even though the scope of that event exceeded the scope of their plans by orders of magnitude.[12]

Beyond planning to reduce the impact of an incident, planning to reduce the vulnerabilities in specific processes is a separate activity.

It may include business changes, technical changes, or both, depending on the business process affected. For example, managers in a tier-one auto supplier may determine that they can live with a maximum of one hour of downtime in manufacturing systems before a customer's production line is impacted. Any more than an hour would cause the line to shut down, leading to unacceptably high fines and goodwill loss, but reducing the potential maximum outage to less than an hour would produce higher costs than any losses the company would otherwise incur. Working backward, the managers can make a combination of adjustments to reduce the risk, such as protecting IT assets so that an outage is unlikely, ensuring that a backup system is available within thirty minutes of an outage, and adjusting finished-goods inventories to allow a half-hour buffer in case of an outage. A similar analysis on supply chain processes may lead managers to focus on changes such as building tighter contractual requirements with suppliers, reducing dependence on particular suppliers (i.e., diversifying the risk), and requiring suppliers to maintain larger inventories on-site than a leaner process might warrant.

Implement and Test the Plan

Most companies run fire drills at regular intervals, but most test their business continuity plans infrequently, if at all. Comprehensive testing is better than walk-through (or "desktop") testing, but walk-through testing is better than none. The muscles developed through training and testing are often surprisingly strong and flexible. No one at the Tata Consultancy Services offices in Mumbai, India, had ever dreamed that a local disaster would shut down two separate company facilities at the same time. When precisely that happened during severe flooding in July 2005, a well-trained Tata incident response team knew how and in what order to contact and coordinate the efforts of key company executives and resources, and the team was able to improvise methods to resume operations for the company's critical outsourcing customers quickly.[13] The Tata team ordered equipment beyond its normal authorization levels, adjusted staff roles on the fly, and worked with customers to quickly develop service alternatives. Team members knew what they had to achieve, and they knew management would back them up. Experience gained in testing and training was the source of that confidence.

Building and testing a continuity plan is a lot of work for enterprises large and small. But BCM directly addresses risks whose severity can otherwise be utterly catastrophic. And by addressing availability risks—the base of the IT risk pyramid—BCM has benefits beyond avoiding catastrophes. For example, in our survey, enterprises that created and tested business continuity plans reported statistically significantly lower levels of agility risk, so they reaped extra value from their BCM investment.

Starting with BCM is a logical first step in improving the foundation—it reduces the impact of risk incidents while generating additional business value. But at the same time, firms should take steps to reduce the likelihood of incidents by identifying and plugging holes in the foundation.

Find and Plug the Holes in the Dike

We all know the story of the brave little Dutch boy (the "hero of Haarlem") who used his finger to plug a hole in the dike that protected his city until help could arrive. This simple, timely action prevented the dike from collapsing and saved the town. Much more work was necessary to rebuild the dike, but if the little Dutch boy hadn't quickly implemented his stopgap solution, there would have been nothing left to fix and no town to save.

Many IT foundations are full of minor holes that may not seem very important, especially to people who are so used to them that they've stopped thinking about them as a problem. Over time, these minor leaks, such as sloppy management of access to systems and data and uncontrolled or undocumented changes in applications, undermine the foundation. All it takes is a hard shove, and the whole structure falls down. A relevant example is the largest reported case of identity theft before 2004. That crime was carried out by an employee of a small financial services company who took advantage of gaps in his company's access management procedures to steal thirty thousand complete credit histories from Experian Corporation's databases over a three-year period.[14] A small gap in procedure became a major problem when a corrupt employee recognized the opportunity and seized it.

Stop the Slop

The most important factor in closing gaps is management attention, and that attention represents additional costs and effort, especially if it's something new for the enterprise. But the potential cost of inattention is much greater than the ongoing cost of crisp execution. A company with at least a hundred thousand customer accounts to protect might spend as much as $16 per customer account in the first year on protections such as data encryption, intrusion prevention, and strong security audits, with costs per account declining proportionately as the number of accounts rises into the millions.[15] That may not sound cheap, but costs typically exceed $90 per customer account if the account data is "cracked," and legislation that is now under consideration in the U.S. Congress to mandate minimum fines for privacy violations could raise these costs to catastrophic levels— up to $11,000 per exposed customer account.[16] Clearly, prevention is less expensive than after-the-fact recovery.

The first step in plugging holes is to find them, and an important means to that end is an internal or external IT audit, which we will soon describe in more detail. But even before an IT audit is under way, the enterprise can look through its recent past, and poll IT and business managers, for warning signs: incidents whose consequences might have been severe if it had not been for luck and circumstance. ChoicePoint's inadvertent sale of more than a hundred fifty thousand personal records to data thieves in February 2005, for example, was presaged by a similar but much less notorious incident in 2002.[17] By the time of the second incident, California had implemented a law (State Bill 1386) that required immediate notification to those California residents whose unencrypted personal information had been subjected to unauthorized access, and ChoicePoint had no choice but to disclose the theft publicly.

In other words, if your enterprise has recently dodged a bullet, it's a good idea to check the condition of your bulletproof vest. It's not a bad idea to keep track of the bullets that are fired at other enterprises, too. The risk officer in a major pharmaceutical firm starts each budget request with a list of recent high-profile IT risks incidents that happened to other firms. This helps remind her bosses that risk management is a relatively small investment that prevents much greater ills. Common baseline safeguards include:

- Ensuring that your organization knows all the infrastructure it owns, understands what business processes each piece of technology supports, and knows how to restore service if the technology fails (these are, of course, elements of BCM—so there's yet another benefit of doing BCM in parallel with finding holes in the dike)

- Holding infrastructure managers accountable for monitoring and maintaining all parts of the infrastructure

- Ensuring that all equipment, including hardware and software, gets software patches, upgrades, and maintenance quickly and safely

- Putting tracking mechanisms in place to show that the previous safeguards are operating effectively

Conduct an IT Audit

The most thorough way to identify the leaks that can produce sudden collapse is to audit IT processes and systems for risk. An IT risk audit, like any other kind of audit, is an independent review of the status of processes and facilities from a qualified expert. The review can be conducted by internal or external auditors—both have advantages and drawbacks.

Enterprises can do IT audits on their own, but they are usually better off using an outside firm for the first audit. An external IT audit costs more than an internal audit, but external auditors bring experience and a measure of impartiality (and credibility) that few firms can generate internally on their first IT audit exercise.

Every enterprise big enough to have internal auditors, even those for whom external auditors are required by regulation, should eventually develop an internal IT audit capability as well. It's not just a matter of cost; our survey analysis shows that internal audit is as effective in reducing overall IT risk as external audit and that it's *more* effective in reducing accuracy risks. Why? Executives tell us that internal auditors have the advantage of an intrinsic level of trust that external auditors can't match. This advantage allows internal auditors to be more proactive than external auditors in exploring risks. For example, internal auditors are often able to dig deeper into projects and, therefore, help project managers avoid risky decisions. Internal auditors also have a broad, ingrained view of enterprise history, strategy, and practices that would take an external auditor years to acquire. Several executives told us that engaging internal auditors early in the life of systems development projects helped them find and fix potential risks before those risks were hardwired into enterprise systems and business processes. (See "Common IT Security and Risk Audit Findings.")

Common IT Security and Risk Audit Findings

Gartner research provided this list of common IT security and risk audit findings, their meanings, and ways to avoid these findings in an audit. Most such findings are related to access and availability, in that order, which is not surprising given the context for the audits. Also not surprising is that proposed remedies in many cases include recommendations for more frequent audits. This is reasonable and fair until a track record of improved controls is established.[a]

Access

1. Typical finding: Business partner agreements and third-party contracts do not specifically address data protection requirements; auditors were unable to obtain a cumulative list of all third-party relationships or evidence of internal controls.

   What it means: Auditors have recognized partners as a significant source of risk in the absence of controls.

   How to avoid it:

   - Minimum—Review third-party contracts for security and risk requirements.

   - Recommended—Require third parties to present evidence of controls and conduct annual reviews. Add security and risk language to contracts.

   - Above and beyond—Require SAS 70 Type 2 audits or equivalent external review and attestation of controls.

2. Typical finding: Auditors were unable to obtain formal evidence that employees have read and understood their responsibilities for data protection.

What it means: Lack of awareness opens the door to a myriad of ills, as described in more detail in chapter 6.

How to avoid it:

- Minimum—Create a manual for users and make it available.

- Recommended—Formalize your training program with formal instruction and professionally produced materials.

- Above and beyond—Establish computer-based training with completion tracking and reporting. Set goals for compliance.

3. Typical finding: Too many administrative or root accounts not tied to individuals.

What it means: Accounts are not bound to a single identity, so your access controls and monitoring tools will not be effective.

How to avoid it:

- Minimum—Remove all shared accounts. Establish policies to prohibit account sharing. Create individual privileged accounts for administrators.

- Recommended—Reduce the number of privileged accounts and administrators.

- Above and beyond—Track all administrator activity.

4. Typical finding: Unable to determine list of privileges for each user. Unable to determine that each user has appropriate privileges approved by granting authority matching the job role.

What it means: There are no controls over who has access to what, and whether that access is approved by an appropriate authority.

How to avoid it:

- Minimum—Establish processes to create users and remove users.

(continued)

- Recommended—Set up automated user provisioning/deprovisioning and identity auditing.

- Above and beyond—Establish role management, privilege attestation, enterprise separation-of-duties detection, and remediation.

5. Typical finding: Unable to track user activity to produce a list of who touched what and when. No evidence of log collection and analysis.

    What it means: Inability to monitor who has accessed specific resources such as databases and files means inability to control or investigate access.

    How to avoid it:

- Minimum—Manually collect and review logs on critical systems.

- Recommended—Implement automated log centralization and analysis.

- Above and beyond—Implement full identity management, database activity monitoring, forensics, and log archiving (and restore!).

6. Typical finding: Unable to produce inventory of information assets and associated classifications.

    What it means: You don't know what information you have, and you don't know how it should be protected.

    How to avoid it:

- Minimum—Create an ad hoc list of critical systems and publish a reasonable classification policy. (Warning: a manual classification process will always be dangerously incomplete.)

- Recommended—Conduct an inventory and classification project.

- Above and beyond—Implement formal asset management and seek automated mechanisms to identify previously unrecognized sensitive data, or use mandatory controls to prevent data leakage.

7. Typical finding: Data center access is uncontrolled.

  What it means: Exactly what it says—data center access is uncontrolled.

  How to avoid it:

- Minimum and recommended—Put access policies in place, minimal controls to enforce policy (locks on doors, sign-in sheets, etc.). Keep application developers out!

- Above and beyond—Require proximity cards, complex multifactor authentication, access control tracking integrated with log-in records, video surveillance, etc.

Availability

1. Typical finding: Unable to find current and environmentally relevant business continuity plans or evidence of internal controls requiring periodic update or review of same.

  What it means: Business continuity planning and management are dangerously deficient. Auditors are now more sensitive to this issue in the wake of serious incidents such as the 9/11 attacks.

  How to avoid it:

- Minimum—Write a minimal disaster recovery and business continuity plan.

- Recommended—Write a formal plan using best practices. Test your plan.

- Above and beyond—Maintain a hot site with automated failover and fail-back. Annual full failover testing.

(continued)

Accuracy

1. Typical finding: Unable to find evidence of change manage-ment on material systems.

   What it means: There are no controls over changes, so it's impossible to know whether change is introducing inaccuracies.

   How to avoid it:

   - Minimum—Establish separate development, test, and pro-duction environments. Implement change request process.

   - Recommended—Implement change management pro-cesses and best practices.

   - Above and beyond—Implement full change management database with configuration auditing and automated change reconciliation.

2. Typical finding: Unable to control issues of segregation of duties in material ERP systems related to financial reporting.

   What it means: Someone could materially affect the integrity of financial reporting through the use of conflicting permissions.

   How to avoid it:

   - Minimum—Manually go through all your ERP users to de-termine if they have conflicting permissions.

   - Recommended—Automate the detection and remediation processes as well as workflow in the provisioning process to prevent further issues.

   - Above and beyond—Continuously monitor ERP transactions for risky use of conflicting permissions.

Source: Paul Proctor and Gartner Risk and Compliance Research Community, March 2007.

a. Note that, given the source—security audits—most of these findings and controls focus on access risks. A full IT audit would cover technology, policy, procedure, and skills relating to all four IT risks: availability, access, accuracy, and agility.

Implement Controls and Audits Based on Standard Frameworks

Controls can be a difficult issue for an enterprise not accustomed to any controls at all—which is the case for many IT organizations. COBIT (Control Objectives for Information and related Technology), an increasingly popular standard for IT processes (including governance and operations management), has 34 major IT process controls and 215 minor ones.[18] Which of these is most important for your enterprise? Which of the 10 major controls related to planning and organizing, or the 13 major controls related to delivery and support, are most urgent? It's impossible to say without knowing what your most significant vulnerabilities are. For this reason, all but the best-funded and most risk-sensitive enterprises implement controls based on audit results, addressing the most serious control issues first before moving on to the others.

Although controls may be designed and built internally, there are many good reasons to use industry-standard frameworks such as COBIT, ITIL (the Information Technology Infrastructure Library), or ISO 17799 (widely recognized as a baseline standard for information security management).[19] Controls are not simple, especially when developing them from scratch. If poorly designed and implemented, they can cause more problems than they solve. Standard industry controls offer many advantages over internally designed controls:

- Implementing a standard framework gives enterprises the benefit of external experts who have learned from the experiences of early adopters.

- Standard controls make benchmarking performance easier because firms can compare numbers on an apples-to-apples basis with others that use the same frameworks.

- Standard frameworks make external audit easier, less expensive, and more accurate because auditors know the frameworks and have experience auditing them.

These advantages notwithstanding, as of this writing, adoption of IT-specific standard frameworks such as COBIT and ITIL is still limited, though increasing. A study (see figure 3-3) shows that in 2005, less than half (45 percent) of all organizations surveyed used a standard process or controls framework for IT governance. One-third of respondents used internally developed frameworks, followed by ISO 9000 at 21 percent, ITIL at 13 percent, and COBIT at 9 percent. Twenty-two percent of respondents had not decided on any framework, which we interpret to mean that the condition of their IT foundations is questionable. Even the 33 percent using internally developed frameworks could benefit by comparing their

FIGURE 3-3

Adoption of standard process and controls frameworks

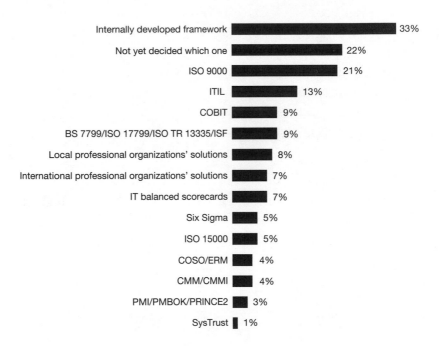

custom frameworks to industry standards to see whether their own frameworks really represent an improvement.[20]

It's a tough job to fix the roof while it's raining, and many enterprises are too busy trying to deal with the results of immature IT processes to devote resources to improving them. In other words, implementing any control framework is not easy. Yet the benefits of a mature, standards-driven IT process are significant, and using an immature process can be very costly indeed. Experience in mitigating project risk via project management methodology is a relevant example. A Gartner process maturity study in the late 1990s, based on data from over seventeen thousand IT projects of various sizes, found that the average organization increased software development productivity by 30 percent in two years by consistently using a moderately rigorous standard process for application development.[21] Having a mature process did more than save costs; it also reduced the number of errors and unpleasant surprises.

Managing business continuity, stopping the slop, auditing IT, and implementing controls and industry best practices are essential steps every enterprise should take to strengthen the base of the risk pyramid. Implementing these mechanisms will significantly reduce the likelihood of incidents and exposure to catastrophic risks while improving the enterprise's capacity to manage risks on an ongoing basis.

The job isn't done when these steps are completed. The highest payoffs in terms of business value and risk reduction (especially in accuracy and agility) result from thorough simplification of the IT installed base, starting with infrastructure. That critically important step is the subject of our next chapter.

Four

Fixing the Foundation

Simplifying the Installed Base

I N CHAPTER 3, we described the initial steps every enterprise should take to bring the foundation up to a competent level. In this chapter we discuss the next step: reducing risk in
the foundation by simplifying infrastructure and applications. Rapid,
thorough simplification of the foundation in one step is not for everyone, especially if the legacy of applications is large, complex, and
business critical. But some simplification is possible for almost any
enterprise—and unlike most spending on risk reduction, in this case
ROI arguments are easily developed and thoroughly compelling.

A rationalized infrastructure reduces risk significantly, and as described in chapter 3, the resulting reduction in costs alone is so compelling that any discussion of risk reduction in the business case is
little more than icing on the cake. Given the financial payoffs, few enterprises can afford *not* to simplify the infrastructure.

Before we get into specifics, however, remember our definition from earlier: *infrastructure* is the platform of shared IT resources, processes, policies, and people that allows business applications to be delivered reliably. It includes computers and other types of hardware, networks, nonbusiness-process-specific applications (such as operating systems, e-mail, and word processors), and common support functions (such as an IT help desk). In many enterprises it also includes standardized applications, such as financial systems or HR, that are shared across the enterprise. (Figure 4-1 depicts infrastructure and its relationship to business strategy, business processes, and applications.)

The Past Weighs Heavy on the Foundation

If only infrastructure simplification was all that is required to simplify the installed base, this would be a short and cheerful chapter indeed! Unfortunately, enterprises have applications on top of their infrastructures—and these applications present an entirely different sort of problem. While infrastructure is often invisible to everyone but the technicians who maintain it, applications are inextricably linked with business processes. Change in infrastructure is technology change; change in applications is business change.

It's difficult for most enterprises to replace an inventory of applications that represents enormous capital investment and a way of doing business that's deeply embedded in the fabric of the enterprise. The decision is even more difficult if those applications apparently support the business more or less adequately. A full makeover of the application portfolio requires very significant capital investment and business change in addition to the necessary technology changes. Further, massive transformation projects can and do fail, leaving the business in the same fix as before (or even worse, as in

FIGURE 4-1

Infrastructure in context

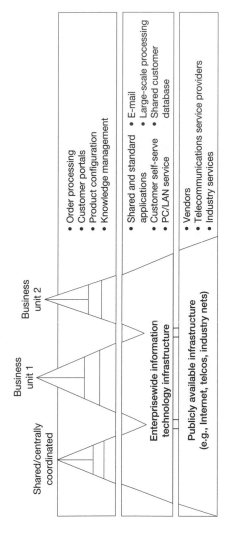

Source: Peter Weill, Mani Subramani, and Marianne Broadbent, "Building IT Infrastructure for Strategic Agility," *MIT Sloan Management Review* 44, no. 1 (2002). Used with permission.

the case of FoxMeyer, a pharmaceutical distributor whose bankruptcy in 1996 followed a failed ERP implementation).[1]

In other words, the business must balance the risks and potential costs of simplifying applications against the risks of living with the legacy. One way to balance the risks is via the pace of transformation.

Enterprises Choose One of Two Paths to Simplify the Foundation

Transformation can proceed in one of two ways: fast and furious, or slow but sure. When legacy risks are already intolerably high, rapid and thorough transformation of applications is more likely. When the constraints imposed on the business by legacy applications are less severe, or when the business has doubts about its ability to control the risks of rapid transformation, simplifying the applications proceeds more slowly.

Rapid Transformation Is Effective but Risky

Tektronix is a good example of rapid transformation driven by the risk of the old.[2] The firm's inability to make a major strategic move proved to senior management that the agility risks of its legacy application base were intolerable. With other major strategic moves sure to come, the senior team was ready to provide funding, attention, and support for a transformation project. CFO Carl Neun and CIO Jim Vance leveraged the success of an infrastructure consolidation that was already under way to lay the groundwork for additional transformation. To further reduce risk on this $55 million three-year initiative, Neun and Vance implemented it in waves—first proving the design, technology, and organization changes behind new uniform global processes and supporting applications in a single division, and only integrating the other two business units when success was achieved in the first. Throughout the transformation, Neun and Vance insisted that each business unit use standard processes and technology. Necessary customizations (e.g., to display text in the local language, or to accommodate multiple currencies) were built as self-contained wrappers riding on top of the standard application.

Ensuring standardization was a tremendous political and organizational challenge that required support from all levels. It paid off in terms of lower risk for all 4A's, especially the accuracy and agility risks that were most important to business executives. Besides successfully divesting the division, Tektronix lowered its other IT risks significantly and improved the overall performance of the business (as described in more detail in the introduction).[3]

Incremental Change Is Slower but Surer

For Tektronix, the risk of radical transformation was lower than the agility risk of continuing to do business on legacy systems. The risk trade-offs are reversed when risks to availability, access, accuracy, or agility in the business's current foundation have not reached a critical state. The urgency of transformation is greatly reduced, and the relative risks of a rapid application transformation project loom much larger. In these cases, enterprises take an incremental approach to improving the foundation.

An unusually patient example of the slow-but-steady approach is Amerada Hess, a $13 billion company in the oil and natural gas industry. Amerada Hess simplified the data underlying a wide range of applications in a major division over a ten-year period, one application at a time, beginning in the mid-1990s.[4] Each new project removed old, nonstandard data structures and replaced them with new standardized, well-architected databases, gradually creating consistent information sources throughout the division. A change in executive management ultimately provided the opportunity to dramatically increase the pace of change. Although the path to simplification was long, the careful groundwork laid over a decade made the final push to the finish line rapid and complete. (We will discuss this case in more detail later in the chapter.)

Successful Foundation Transformations Follow Three Steps

Although the fast-and-furious and slow-but-steady approaches have different risk/benefit profiles, they follow a common three-step sequence:

1. Both approaches start with a clear architectural vision that serves as a guide to the transformation—a compass and a rudder, as described later in this chapter.

2. They proceed by improving infrastructure to reduce risk at the base of the risk pyramid, cut operations costs, and provide a solid platform for the rebuilt applications.

3. With a robust platform in place and a clear direction, the tough challenge of transforming legacy applications then begins.

The three steps sometimes overlap, and some enterprises do one or more steps faster than others, but the winning sequence remains the same.

The ongoing foundation simplification program at the U.S. Department of Housing and Urban Development (HUD) shows this sequence at work.[5] In 1996, the $35 billion agency had a very complex, costly, and risky foundation. Three primary business functions (housing, community development, and public housing) had been established under separate legislative mandates, were regulated by different congressional committees, and operated very independently—they even had separate business-unit-based IT staffs. Independence, topped by legislative mandates that demanded fast action but not well-structured IT systems, resulted in a poorly structured IT foundation, one that was fragmented, costly to support, and inflexible. "We have a plan to migrate our major legacy systems to modern platforms by 2010," HUD CIO Lisa Schlosser told us, "because they constrain the business. They consist of millions of lines of code built over twenty years, and they are very inflexible."

HUD first assessed its technology portfolio against business needs to develop its architectural plan by (1) dividing the IT technology portfolio by lines of business; (2) identifying the core business and support processes for HUD and each line of business; (3) mapping all IT systems against these functions; and, finally, (4) developing a plan and architecture for a streamlined systems environment.

Once analysis and architecture plans were completed, HUD focused on reducing the infrastructure costs that accounted for the majority of its IT budget. Eliminating redundant applications and infrastructure contributed to reducing the IT staff, the largest component of HUD's IT infrastructure costs, by about 25 percent. "We put so many efficiencies in place that we were able to reduce costs significantly, freeing up money for reinvestment," Schlosser told us. Large-scale application replacement—the third stage in the overall simplification—is now under way. Notwithstanding the considerable cost of this third stage, HUD's overall IT budget has remained stable thanks to the groundwork laid in the architecture and infrastructure stages.[6]

Architecture Plots the Course and Keeps the Transformation on Track

It is no accident that defining the architecture is the first step to simplification. (See "What Is an Architecture?" for examples of two companies' architectural visions.) An architecture sets a future vision for business processes and supporting technology and so provides guidance for technology decisions that play out over the course of years.

The same vision, detailed down to the level of highly specific technology standards, is a yardstick for assessing the future value and risk of current enterprise technologies. In this sense, the architecture framework serves as a compass for the journey to a simplified foundation, reducing availability, access, accuracy, and, ultimately, agility risk by preventing unnecessary complexity before it begins.

An architectural vision is implemented via decisions made on every project that the enterprise completes. By systematically aligning new plans and designs with architectural standards, the enterprise "future-proofs" the new environment against unnecessary complexity that increases risk. The reverse is also—sadly—true. As the backstory to the HUD case shows, decisions made without regard for architectural standards are far more likely to increase complexity and risk than to reduce them. Simplicity means limiting choices, but without an architecture, anything goes. In this sense, architecture is a rudder—it keeps the enterprise on course to its destination.

What Is an Architecture?

Enterprise architecture is "the organizing logic for business processes and IT infrastructure, reflecting the integration and standardization requirements of the company's operating model."[a] Effective architectures reflect both the business's vision of how the enterprise's processes should perform and IT's understanding of the technology needed to support that vision. The story can be represented at the highest level on a single page, as MetLife's and ING Direct's enterprise architectures show.

MetLife's architecture, as depicted in the figure, shows shared and standardized technology services (in the middle of the diagram) that connect customer-facing applications ("Application presentation tier") and large shared back-end applications and

MetLife's enterprise architecture

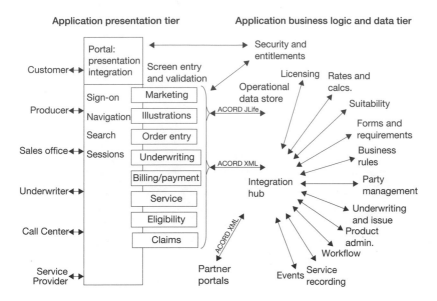

Application presentation tier   Application business logic and data tier

Source: Adapted from MetLife documents. Reprinted from Jeanne Ross, Peter Weill, and David Robertson, *Enterprise Architecture as Strategy: Creating a Foundation for Business Execution* (Boston: Harvard Business School Press, 2006), 59. Used with permission.

databases ("Application business logic and data tier"). This architecture reduces accuracy risk by integrating diverse business processes into an accurate shared view of each customer and account while allowing for the agility to add processes as needed. Availability and access risks are managed at the level of particular processes and tiers.

The architecture of ING Direct, shown in the figure, is highly modular, with different business services (e.g., core banking, customer relationship, external services) that ride on a shared platform of common business and channel services. All information is integrated within each country, but data and systems for each country are separate. The architecture reduces the agility risk of

ING Direct's enterprise architecture

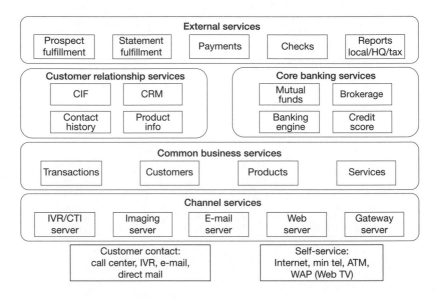

Source: David Robertson, "ING Direct: The IT Challenge (B)," IMD-3-1345 (Lausanne, Switzerland: IMD, 2003). Used with permission.

entering new countries or launching a new product within a country by restraining how much each country-based business can customize its systems. Availability, access, and accuracy risks are reduced within each country by using standardized software.

a. Jeanne W. Ross, Peter Weill, and David C. Robertson, *Enterprise Architecture as Strategy: Creating a Foundation for Business Execution* (Boston: Harvard Business School Press, 2006).

Without architecture, a business has no way to steer a course toward a better-structured foundation and no real way of knowing that what replaces the current foundation will be any better, or less risky, than what it had before. It is difficult for any enterprise to calculate the value of avoiding bad decisions; that said, a well-defined architecture framework, consistently applied, helps an enterprise avoid those bad decisions that inevitably compound over time into an IT foundation that is overly complex, difficult to manage, and riddled with risky holes.

Simplifying Infrastructure Starts the Change and Builds Momentum

Earlier in this chapter and in previous chapters, we described numerous examples of the role of infrastructure in IT risk and the importance of improving infrastructure as an early step in improving the foundation discipline. IT units can typically improve infrastructure on their own, with little or no change required in the business processes. Improving infrastructure reduces the two risks at the bottom of the pyramid—availability and access—while laying the groundwork for application improvements that reduce the higher-level risks of accuracy and agility. Improving infrastructure also pays financial dividends. As we mentioned in chapter 3, the savings can be 10 percent or more of an IT budget, or tens of millions of dollars per year in a large enterprise.

Few enterprises can afford *not* to simplify infrastructure. It reduces costs and reduces risks while building momentum for the more difficult job of restructuring applications. Most enterprises can make significant improvements right now by *rationalizing* their infrastructure—moving to a planned and managed set of standardized components, and reducing the sheer number of components by sharing resources and removing redundant assets. This is typically done in three steps:

1. *Centralization:* consolidating infrastructure resources into fewer data centers, with more centralized management

2. *Standardization:* using fewer types and versions of hardware and software

3. *Rationalization:* moving to less hardware and less software, with more sharing of resources between business units, less duplication, and fewer inefficiencies (a common example is sharing disaster recovery capacity among services)[7]

For example, Tektronix rationalized its infrastructure by using these methods. Before the application transformation began, Tektronix had already centralized seven separate data centers, which were running a variety of mainframe and minicomputers from multiple vendors, to three data centers and then to one. In 1996, the company standardized with Unix minicomputers as the platform that would host the transformed applications and outsourced all operations not related to minicomputers to a third party. Similarly, Tektronix had already standardized a network that consisted of a jumble of communications technologies, lines, and converters into a global network based entirely on the Internet protocol (or "IP") communications standard. The new network was vastly easier to manage, monitor, and expand, and it easily handled growth from approximately twenty global sites to more than a hundred. These infrastructure rationalization efforts dramatically reduced the complexity, cost, and risk of the foundation even *before* the applications were transformed.[8]

Finish Fixing the Foundation by Simplifying Applications—Carefully

Many CIOs advise us that their custom-built legacy applications are 30–50 percent more expensive to maintain and operate than their packaged systems or other newer technologies. That cost, and the increased opportunity cost it implies, is a constant pain to the IT team, but when a business executive compares it to the high business and IT costs of change, it often seems slight.

The decision to replace an important legacy application is almost always based on business risk and value, not on IT costs. It is made either when the threat of catastrophic failure is imminent or constraints on the business model are too severe to tolerate the status quo any longer, as was the case with Tektronix's transformation. In other words, the tipping point for legacy application change arrives only when the business risk of keeping an application clearly exceeds the business value of the processes it supports.

In the worst cases, the benefit/risk tipping point passes unrecognized, or it is resisted until a catastrophic failure is imminent or actually realized. Such failures are as unnecessary as they are dangerous. Practically *no* legacy application crisis—with few exceptions—arrives without warning. The circumstances that increase risk and reduce value are almost always visible—often years before the tipping point is reached.

Business Cases for Legacy Migration Are Based on Value and Risk

There are three essential business cases for replacing a legacy application, and they are defined by their mix of value and risk (see figure 4-2):

1. A business case based on *value* is aimed at improving business performance in terms that include revenue and profit; business productivity gain or cost reduction; competitive differentiation and improved market positioning; downside business risk reduction (e.g., via compliance with regulation); or improved business agility.

2. A business case based on *risk* is about the potential for business process failure, caused either by an outright technology failure or by the failure of the supporting technology to meet changing business needs. Common factors that precipitate intolerable risk include the retirement or departure of the personnel maintaining the technology, the termination of vendor support for the platforms or applications, or a change in regulations.

FIGURE 4-2

Value- and risk-based business cases for legacy application replacement

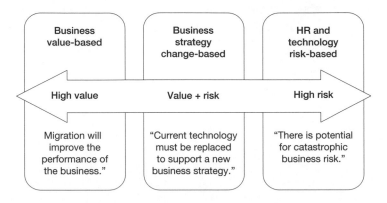

Business value-based	Business strategy change-based	HR and technology risk-based
High value	Value + risk	High risk
Migration will improve the performance of the business."	"Current technology must be replaced to support a new business strategy."	"There is potential for catastrophic business risk."

Source: Richard Hunter and Dave Aron, "High Value, High Risk: Managing the Legacy Portfolio," Research Report (Stamford, CT: Gartner Executive Programs, September 2006).

3. A business case based on combined *value and risk* is usually appropriate when business strategy is changing. A change in business strategy, whether driven internally or by market demands, often requires new capabilities in both business processes and the information systems that support them. The technology risk in this case may not be catastrophic; it's enough that there is significant potential for damage to the strategy through the legacy systems' failure to support new business requirements.[9]

The key to managing the legacy portfolio, and the risk it embodies, is to periodically assess and compare value and risk over time. By doing so, enterprises get plenty of warning before the tipping point arrives, so they can systematically increase the value of their application base while reducing its inherent risks.

For some companies, such as Tektronix or Celanese (discussed in chapter 6), the risks posed by the legacy base were so high—especially in terms of accuracy and agility—and the benefits of better accuracy and agility were so palpable that they could make the case for a fast-and-furious replacement project. However, the risks are less obvious in most cases, and most enterprises must be more patient. By opportunistically piggybacking on business changes, opportunities, and risks, these enterprises shape each new project to move the firm gradually in the direction of the architectural vision. Architecture is the compass and rudder for this journey, but CIOs and their teams are the pilots.

Amerada Hess Mastered the Slow-but-Steady Approach

The slow-but-steady approach used by Amerada Hess is a remarkable example of patient architecture-driven planning combined with opportunistic action.[10] The information structures embedded in applications were numerous and nonstandardized, difficult to combine and integrate, resulting in high accuracy and agility risks. To put it another way, it was very difficult for anyone to know for sure that the information behind a tough decision was up-to-date and accurate. On the other hand, overall business perception of risk was low—as is common when managers and employees have lived with certain risks for a very long time—and there was no support for a fast-and-furious restructuring of the application base.

CIO Richard Ross and his team used a combination of patience, planning, and negotiation to move the firm incrementally along the right path, guided by architecture. According to Ross, "In the beginning, we found one savvy business user in finance, so we started to implement the architecture in the middle, building a data mart layer one application at a time."[11] He further explained, "When there were requests for systems, we told the project teams the benefit of spending a little bit more to get something much better"—a system whose standardized data structure and ensured accuracy provided a much more timely and accurate basis for business decisions.

Ross and his team soon found that technical complexities were much less of a barrier to simplification than fundamental disagreements between business units on the meaning of business terms. For example, one business unit interpreted the words *volume sold* as referring to a forecast; another thought it referred to the quantity of product delivered to buyers. "We brought these parties together and asked them to reconcile their definitions," Ross told us. "Many of them had been using their personal spreadsheets to forecast. We got them to agree on one data source and one meaning [for each term]. That got us common definitions of data. Once we reached critical mass, we could show the value."

As is typical of risks (like accuracy) that lie higher on the IT risk pyramid, these changes had impacts on the organization that went beyond technology issues. Ross explained what happened at Amerada Hess: "We sat down with management teams and talked about what actions they would take on the data on their screens—such as what they might do when a block of data is highlighted in red, indicating a critical situation. We worked up a set of operating principles so that everyone would be clear about whom an executive might call for answers and what actions [those management teams] might take. These operating principles helped people lower in the organization who had always been afraid of providing data for management for fear of how it might be used."

The gradual approach took Amerada Hess a long way on its journey. It also positioned the firm to leapfrog the last few steps. In 2002, a new division president set a priority to manage the business via a simplified, consistent, divisionwide set of numbers. The new president's previous company had paid $100 million to achieve that kind of integrated reporting, and he was willing to pay the same price, if necessary, in this case. But because the emerging architecture at Amerada Hess was already proven in multiple applications and had strong support from business executives and managers who had already benefited from the gradual transformation, the IT group could confidently propose a one-year conversion for all remaining databases at a cost of $10 million. The groundwork laid application by application came to rapid fruition, significantly reducing accuracy and agility risks throughout the division—an overnight success ten years in the making.

The Tipping Point for Risk and Value Can Be Forecast Years in Advance

Where applications are concerned, business value and business risk usually evolve over time in largely predictable ways. They are affected by external factors, such as changing business conditions, as well as internal factors, like resource availability or a change in business strategy. Many of these factors have visibility that extends well into the future, and enterprises can often estimate and compare risk and value with reasonable accuracy years in advance. Such estimates can be used to determine whether and when the business should consider replacing a given system.

Forecasting trends in business value. Value resides in a business process, not in the applications that support it.[12] Forecasting future trends in business value, therefore, is done process by process, by asking questions about the role of the process in the enterprise's business proposition and how that role will increase or decrease over time. For example: Is the process part of a high-margin business unit, or is it a cost driver for the business? Will the process (and the business units it supports) grow in importance over time or shrink in significance? What events will trigger these changes? When will that happen?

Different types of value—growth, profitability, cost reduction, regulatory compliance, competitive differentiation, and so on—can be important for different processes and different reasons, and not all are easily quantifiable. But analysts and executives can still use standard checklists or diagnostic questionnaires to estimate relative value within a given category and then weight different types of value appropriately to produce an estimate or index of total value.

Projecting business value numbers several years into the future provides a systematic way to compare within and across processes, year to year.

Forecasting trends in application risk. Value resides in business processes, but IT risk resides in the legacy applications. Just as firms can perform reasonably accurate forecasts for value years into the future, they can perform comparable forecasts for risks as well. It's most useful to focus on applications that support high-value business processes; application replacement decisions are rarely difficult when the processes they support have low value. If a business impact analysis (as described in chapter 3) has already been completed as part of business continuity management, then a mapping of applications to processes is already available. If not, one must be created.

Risk is assessed by asking questions about an application's impact on the availability, access, accuracy, and agility of the business processes it supports, now and into the future. Questions include:

- Does the system constrain the business from operating effectively? How?

- Is the system consistent with current and planned architectural standards? Can it be modified as necessary to meet changing business needs (e.g., by scaling up capacity as needed)?

- Does the system perform with adequate reliability? What is the potential for technical failure and its likely business consequences?

- Are controls sufficient to meet legal and internal policy requirements?

- Is the system's resource consumption, including human resources, acceptable?

- Are adequate human resources to support it available internally or externally?

- Is the system well documented?

- Is the software and hardware currently supported by the vendors involved?

- How will the answers to the questions asked so far change in the foreseeable future?

- What events will drive these changes? When will these events occur?

By using a defined rating scheme and weighting different types of risk according to the enterprise's tolerance for each, the enterprise can systematically compare overall risk estimates application by application and year by year.

Although in risk assessments IT managers tend to emphasize the technical quality of applications, technical quality is a decisive factor only when it is so poor that it threatens the effectiveness of a business process. In general, risks that greatly constrain or threaten the business—such as the inability to support new business initiatives (agility), the potential for a catastrophic system failure (availability), or the likelihood of regulatory sanctions (accuracy or access)—must be weighted most heavily. For example, a system's inability to scale to higher capacity levels is a high-priority availability risk when forecasts show that business growth is likely to require a higher capacity in the foreseeable future, but not when business growth is forecasted to be slow or stagnant.

Forecasting risk relative to value. The final step in the assessment process is to overlay time lines for value and risk (see figure 4-3). It's not necessary to match the scales for value and risk precisely; it's enough to compare the shapes of the risk and value lines. When risk

FIGURE 4-3

Application risk and value time line

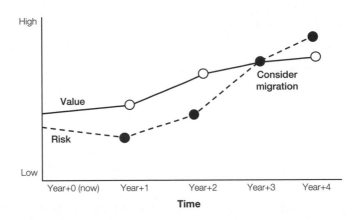

Source: Richard Hunter and Dave Aron, "High Value, High Risk: Managing the Legacy Portfolio," Research Report (Stamford, CT: Gartner Executive Programs, September 2006).

rises sharply relative to value, it's time to consider replacing the system. That shift may result from an increase in risk, perhaps caused by events (such as a major regulatory change or an expansion in market demand that will exceed system capacity), or from a decrease in business process value (such as one that might occur after a divestment, a decision to "sunset" a product line, or an increase in competitor capabilities). Charting risk and value over time gives the enterprise an idea of how long it has to plan and execute migration—or to reduce the risk to acceptable levels.

At Amcor, an Australian paper manufacturer, 50 percent of the IT personnel assigned to maintain the aging mission-critical application that controlled paper mill operations retired en masse in January 2006. According to Amcor CIO Rob Pyne, "You'd better believe it was a nontrivial event."[13] Because the event was foreseeable well in advance, Pyne was able to mitigate the impact of the team's departure by carefully building expertise in his remaining personnel. But the event was a clear indicator that the risk-to-value ratio of the aging technology—whose life has already been extended with add-ons like third-party reporting systems—had changed. At some point *all* the personnel working on the system will be gone. The value of the business process remains high, but the level of availability and agility risk is rising fast. Pyne is already preparing proposals for replacing the technology.

Revisiting risk and value assessments annually helps enterprises avoid being blindsided by an application risk that suddenly becomes catastrophic, and it allows enterprises to make the appropriate business case for application change at the moment that's right for the business. Over time, the application base improves incrementally and opportunistically, with less organizational trauma (albeit at a much slower pace) than a radical fast-and-furious replacement.

Develop a Reinvestment Plan and Renewal Budget

Regardless of whether you choose a fast-and-furious or slow-but-steady approach, it's important to ensure that the risk removed from the foundation at great effort and expense does not return. Systematically reinvesting in legacy renewal is an important means to that end. A typical approach to systematic renewal treats hardware and software as assets to be replaced on a schedule that avoids business reliance on obsolescent technology. Since price-performance ratios of technology improve rapidly, such replacements upgrade business performance without increasing cost.

At Foreign Affairs and International Trade (FAIT) Canada, a public agency, CIO Pierre Sabourin uses a renewal fund equal to 20 percent of the IT budget as a tool to encourage business units to continuously simplify and upgrade their infrastructure and applications.[14] A few basic rules guide FAIT's cyclical upgrade efforts: PCs are replaced every four years, and printers are replaced every six. Software is retired when the vendors drop support for the product in question or when the product no longer fits within the agency's architecture footprint.

Sabourin and his staff start to consider replacing or upgrading an application once it's five years old. But making the case to change an application is rarely simple. According to Sabourin, "Applications are not commodities like PCs. Business owners of applications don't have a life cycle culture. They only see the up-front costs to build, not the ongoing costs to maintain. And business managers who are P&L-driven don't have long-term incentives to keep a platform upgraded."

Sabourin's solution is the CIO Fund—a portion of the cyclical replacement budget, approved by senior managers, that can be allocated to funding, simplifying, and renewing particular applications as needed. "It's the honey that attracts the bees—that is, the people who are falling behind. I can use the CIO Fund to pay business unit owners to get off an old platform. It's a new idea for us, but already the business units love it."

No enterprise can ignore the foundation discipline. For the fortunate few that begin with a green field or those enterprises that have reached a turning point in business strategy that requires a new and drastically improved technology platform, a foundation of simplified, standardized, and well-managed infrastructure and applications can serve as the focal discipline for risk management.

In most enterprises, years of locally optimized technology deployment without a clear architectural guidance has produced an environment whose complexity and tight connection to business process make radical simplification extremely difficult and costly. In such an environment, the foundation discipline has great value, but carrying it to its logical extreme is a practical impossibility. Instead, these enterprises need to bring the foundation up to a competent level as soon as possible by identifying and plugging leaks in the

dike, ending sloppy execution, adding basic IT controls, and im
menting business continuity management. Then they can start the
wheels rolling to simplify and improve infrastructure and applications over time.

In such complex, unwieldy legacy environments, the focal discipline for IT risk management is likely to be the risk governance process
or awareness. Because process is so often the focus of risk management
efforts in large complex companies and is often underemphasized in
smaller resource-constrained companies, we'll address the discipline of
risk governance process in our next chapter.

Five

Developing the Risk Governance Process

A FUNDAMENTAL ISSUE in risk management is that the people who can best prioritize risk management across the enterprise are the least likely to be able to identify and address the risks. Executives can very effectively make business trade-offs among risks and assign funding and responsibility to address risks. But they do not have the detailed knowledge of each unit that is required to identify the risks, nor do they have the time or skills to address the risks. Detailed operational knowledge and skills are usually found much lower in the organization, with people who tend to have a limited view of the whole enterprise and thus cannot make effective enterprisewide trade-offs.

Coming to a true understanding of an enterprise's risks is like the East Indian folktale of the blind men meeting an elephant for the first time. One blind man grabs the elephant's trunk and says, "The elephant is like a snake." A second touches the elephant's leg and says, "The elephant is like a tree." A third takes hold of the elephant's tail and announces, "The elephant is like a rope." A fourth feels the elephant's side and says, "No, no! The elephant is like a wall!" All the blind men are partly right, and all are mostly wrong. Unless they figure out some way to share what they have discovered, none of them will ever have a clear idea of what an elephant is really like. That will be a problem if they ever have to deal with a rampaging elephant.

Like the four blind men, enterprises need a way to link fragmented views of the IT risk "elephant" to develop an accurate, comprehensive, shared, and action-oriented picture of all IT risks. Beyond integrating information about risk, enterprises must also have a way to resolve legitimate disagreements about the likelihood and impact of each risk (see the box "What Every Parent Knows About Risk Management").

Getting a comprehensive and consistent picture of risks, keeping them up-to-date, and then acting on them appropriately is a dif-

---

What Every Parent Knows About Risk Management

Imagine that George's four-year old daughter, Clare, is on the jungle gym at the local playground. She climbs about three feet off the ground and calls, "Hey, Daddy! Look at me!" George, of course, says, "Go higher!" He is, after all, concerned about Clare's agility risk—he wants her to grow up to be the most confident, capable woman she can be. George's wife, Marilyn, on the other hand, says, "You're already too high. Come down a bit." Marilyn is concerned about a different risk—namely, availability; if Clare falls, she may not live to need agility as an adult.

ficult task in most enterprises. But there is a way to do it. The answer is the second IT risk management discipline—the risk governance process—which we describe in this chapter. With an effective IT risk governance process, executives at all levels have the information they need to make and implement smart, confident business decisions about which IT risks to reduce, which to avoid, which to transfer (via insurance, outsourcing or other means), and which to live with. Without a risk governance process, enterprises cannot understand the real extent and nature of the risks they face, which leaves them vulnerable to unpleasant surprises.

The Need for an IT Risk Governance Process at PFPC

When Michael Harte became PFPC's first enterprisewide CIO in 2001, information technology in this $800 million financial services provider, which administered $1.7 trillion in assets, was highly fragmented—

After extensive discussions, George and Marilyn resolved the difference in their risk priorities. Clare can climb higher than Marilyn would allow if George is there to catch her in case she falls.

If risk prioritization is so difficult in this context, when both parties have only their daughter's best interests at heart, consider how much more difficult it is to reach consensus on risk in an enterprise full of different objectives and hidden agendas.

Just like George and Marilyn, enterprises need a way to manage trade-offs among their key risks. We have found that the risk governance process is the best way for people with different points of view to get a full picture of IT risks and reach consensus on how to address them

---

the result of a decade of rapid growth and acquisitions in ten separate business segments, each with their own IT organizations.[1] Harte was charged with unifying and transforming the firm's fragmented IT assets to reduce cost, improve enterprisewide information visibility, and increase agility. But in the short term, Harte knew that numerous IT risks were present, and the company had no process to manage them.

IT risk was a critical issue to PFPC. The company's business consisted largely of processing transactions for other banks, and timeliness and accuracy were vital to its customers. Furthermore, the company was frequently audited—by Wall Street regulators, banking regulators, and even its clients' auditors. Previous financial restatements by parent company PNC Financial ensured that PNC and its subsidiaries would be under close scrutiny by regulators and clients alike for some time to come.

Harte realized quickly that his firm's biggest IT risk was that he and his colleagues didn't know what their IT risks were. They needed a well-rounded picture of all the IT risks in the enterprise. They also had to find a way to resolve disagreements among Harte's staff and his peers about which risks were most important. Accordingly, Harte chose to make risk management one of the two pillars of his IT transformation plan and to make the risk governance process the program's focal discipline. Throughout the chapter, we will describe how PFPC and other enterprises implemented their risk governance processes.

An Effective, Multilayered IT Risk Governance Process

The challenge for executives is to design and implement a risk governance process that links local risk expertise with central oversight and decision making. In any organization of at least moderate size, no single person can develop an enterprisewide view of IT risks on his own and take the necessary actions based on his assessment. Because of this issue, effective risk management processes and management structures need to be multilayered, giving people at each level the information they need to do their part, without bogging down in complexity and bureaucracy.

Well-designed IT risk governance enables local experts to identify and address risks while enabling executives to see enterprise-wide risks and allocate resources to the most important ones. The multilayered approach has several advantages:

- *It puts knowledge at different levels of the organization to work where it is most effective.* There's as little point in having senior managers make detailed implementation-level decisions about technical standards as there is in having technicians define corporate policy. Both implementation-level decision making and corporate policy are necessary; neither by itself is sufficient.

- *It allows managers to make decisions based on a view of all risks at their level of the organization.* Risks that rank high for a small business unit may be low for the enterprise as a whole. Allowing multiple levels to make decisions about risks at their level ensures that a broader set of risks will be addressed than if all decisions were made at a single level.

- *It provides a ready-made path to escalate disputes.* If disagreements can't be resolved to everyone's satisfaction at the point of origin, a multilevel structure provides a clear path to the next level of authority.

- *It increases awareness of policy and standards at every level of the organization.* The multilevel structure encourages participation in risk governance at every management level in the enterprise, and with participation comes awareness. (We discuss risk awareness at length in the next chapter.)

Roles in the IT Risk Governance Process

The organizational structures for IT risk management include five organizational roles: the executive sponsor, risk policy council, implementation council, IT risk management team, and local managers and experts. Each has an important, but different, responsibility (see figure 5-1). The sixth role, the IT risk officer, ties together the information, decision-making authority, and expertise of the other five roles, and is directly responsible for outcomes. Let's look at all six roles in turn.

FIGURE 5-1

Typical organizational structures in the IT risk governance process

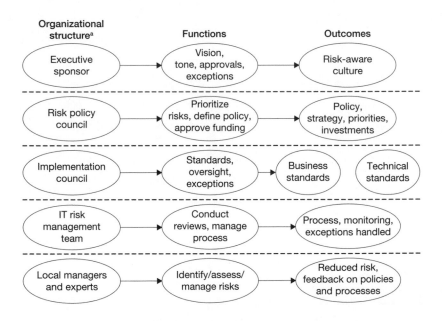

ᵃThe IT risk officer is a key liaison among all these structures.

Executive sponsor. The executive sponsor provides top-down vision and support for IT risk management policy. Among other things, the sponsor sets the tone for risk management in the enterprise, ensuring that the culture is risk aware (see chapter 6) and that all responsible parties are playing their roles in the process. The sponsor often participates in other ways, such as in the risk policy council, and is usually the court of last resort for exception requests. The person filling the sponsor role is often the enterprise COO, CFO, CIO (in a larger organization), or CEO (in a smaller one).

Risk policy council. The risk policy council includes enterprise-level executives (including the enterprise CIO), the IT risk officer, and, in many cases, the corporate counsel and head of human resources. This council sets and reviews policy and enterprise-level priorities for specific risks, approves funding for programs and initiatives aimed at reducing risk, and reviews exceptions that cannot be resolved at lower levels.

Implementation council. A second council, the implementation council, generally consists of business-unit-level managers (including IT managers), direct reports to the members of the executive council, and the IT risk officer, who serves as a key liaison between councils. This council's role is to implement risk management policy via business and technical standards and procedures. Members also ensure that local operational managers and experts conduct periodic risk reviews in consistent ways and prioritize the results of those assessments.

IT risk management team. The detailed work of making the risk management process run falls to the IT risk management (ITRM) team. The ITRM team reports to the IT risk officer and calls on analysts and specialized experts as necessary. In small- and medium-sized

firms, the IT risk management team often relies on part-time commit-
ments from individuals across the organization. In larger organizations the ITRM team is more typically a dedicated team. Even in very
large companies, it's rare for this team to include more than a dozen
members; we have not seen a team with more than thirty full-time
members. The ITRM team creates tools and templates for use at all
levels of the risk governance process; assists local managers and experts to identify and assess risks; and reviews upcoming projects,
operating procedures, and installed applications for compliance to
risk management policies and standards. Members identify when action is needed and initiate processes to formally review exception requests when they can't be avoided or immediately resolved. They also
produce the detailed analysis and reports that higher-level roles use to
monitor the status of the IT risk management program.

Local managers and experts. It's local managers and experts
who identify, assess, and manage specific risks in their business or
functional areas. They are the experts on their units' operations and
future strategies and so are best positioned to understand which
risks need to be addressed. These people identify risks in their units
and prioritize them according to policy established by the risk councils and ITRM team. They manage lower-priority risks on their own
and report higher-priority risks to the implementation council.
Local managers typically resolve most risks on their own, with expert help from the ITRM team or other experts as required.

IT risk officer. The person who is ultimately responsible for the
process of managing IT risk (but not for managing particular risks)
is the IT risk officer. In a large, complex business, the risk manager
position is likely to be full time; in smaller organizations, it may be
part time. The IT risk officer usually reports directly to either the
enterprise CIO or the enterprise risk officer and on a dotted-line
basis to the one she doesn't report to directly.[2] The IT risk officer

ensures that the risk governance process includes contributions from experts in multiple operational areas, that risk is assessed from various viewpoints, and that a history of risks is established to allow the enterprise to track progress and trends.

We reviewed various listings in risk management forums to learn more about the responsibilities of the IT risk officer. These duties include:

- Managing a team of IT risk reviewers

- Negotiating, planning, and executing an IT operational review plan in concert with the CIO

- Working with business unit leaders to design processes to address identified IT risks

- Managing special investigations, completion audits, and other projects as necessary

- Coordinating IT risk management efforts with teams at the corporate level and business unit level

- Reporting to the CIO and enterprise risk officer as required

- Determining priorities, recording tasks, delegating assignments, and monitoring time lines

- Building working relationships with business unit leaders and the board

The same sources provided insight into the skills and experience required by the job. Such job descriptions include the following:

- Ability to understand risks and practical control

- Analytical and strategic thinking

- Ability to understand complex legal and regulatory issues

- Professional and discreet personal manner

- Ability to communicate complex issues to business unit leaders clearly

- Ability to lead through persuasion

IT Risk Governance Roles in Practice

Each role in the governance structure may be filled by a single person, a committee, or a number of people working in parallel under the direction of a responsible manager. The exception is the IT risk officer, who should be just one person. In smaller and less complex enterprises, higher- or lower-level roles may be collapsed into a smaller number of councils, but care should be taken when combining policy and implementation councils—the knowledge needed to function effectively in those roles is very different, and few personnel can be effective in both.

In some firms, risk management is a simple structure of information coordination. At a large chemical manufacturer, the corporate risk officer (CRO) and her team develop policy and processes to manage risk across the enterprise, at the behest of the firm's chairman, who fills the executive sponsor role. IT is one of twenty-five functional or business units that participate in the process. Middle managers and staff in each unit fill the role of local managers and experts for their units, identifying risks and assessing them according to policy and templates provided by the risk management team. Each local manager or expert reports risks to the head of the unit, who is responsible for managing the most important twenty or more operational risks in the unit and reporting the top five risks to the CRO. The CRO and her risk management team then prioritize a list of the top twenty risks from the ones they receive and present those risks to the corporate board, which plays the role of executive risk council (see figure 5-2).

PFPC used a more complex structure for IT risk management. CIO Michael Harte assumed the role of executive sponsor and appointed a

FIGURE 5-2

Risk governance role structure at a chemical manufacturer

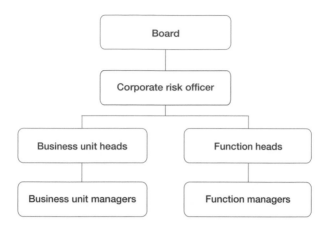

Source: © 2007 MIT Sloan Center for Information Systems Research. Used with permission.

deputy, Kwafo Ofori-Boateng, as the IT risk officer.[3] Ofori-Boateng worked full-time at first to develop and improve the process and risk policy. Later, as the process stabilized, he was able to take on additional responsibilities beyond risk management. He worked with a loosely defined part-time risk management team that consisted of IT and non-IT staff and corporate risk managers. The executive council, which PFPC called the Technology Risk Management Council (TRMC), consisted of Harte's seven reports, each of whom was responsible for a key area of IT management—such as operations, application development, or security—across the firm's ten business segments. The TRMC monitored progress on IT risk and prioritized risk management across the enterprise. IT managers and staff throughout the organization were the local managers and experts who identified and resolved IT risks in their areas. At PFPC the role of the policy council was shared between the IT risk management team and the TRMC.

Figure 5-3 shows how PFPC's IT risk management roles fit within a broader umbrella of risk management at PFPC and its parent company, PNC Financial. PFPC's IT risk process integrated with

FIGURE 5-3

PFPC's technology risk management triangle

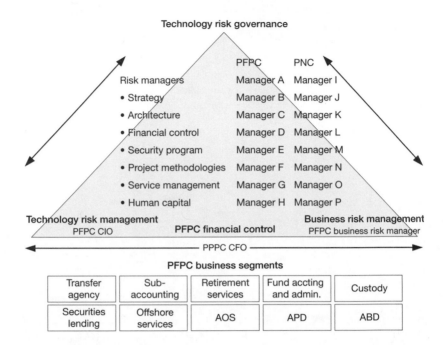

Technology risk governance

	PFPC	PNC
Risk managers	Manager A	Manager I
• Strategy	Manager B	Manager J
• Architecture	Manager C	Manager K
• Financial control	Manager D	Manager L
• Security program	Manager E	Manager M
• Project methodologies	Manager F	Manager N
• Service management	Manager G	Manager O
• Human capital	Manager H	Manager P

Technology risk management
PFPC CIO

PFPC financial control

Business risk management
PFPC business risk manager

◄—————— PPPC CFO ——————►

PFPC business segments

Transfer agency	Sub-accounting	Retirement services	Fund accting and admin.	Custody
Securities lending	Offshore services	AOS	APD	ABD

Source: George Westerman and Robert Walpole, "PFPC: Building and IT Risk Management Competency," working paper 352, Center for Information Systems Research, MIT Sloan School of Management, Cambridge, MA. Used with permission.

Note: Managers' names removed to protect confidentiality.

the firm's business risk management process, which was led by the business risk manager, who convened the enterprise-level Risk Management Committee at the behest of PFPC's CEO. Technology risk governance at PFPC also worked very closely with the same processes at PNC Financial, which consolidated views of risk across its subsidiaries.

Making IT risk a part of an organization's enterprise risk management process is an effective way to ensure that IT risks get the same attention as other business risks. When IT risks are identified and assessed in terms of business impact, it's a straightforward matter to compare them to the rest of the enterprise list, consolidate the lists, and prioritize the IT risks against the others. In a large company, it is not unusual for IT risks to account for five to ten items in a list of fifty to sixty enterprise risks.[4]

Steps in the IT Risk Governance Process

Risks are identified and managed by local managers and experts, who are overseen by the executive sponsor and councils, and the overall process is managed by the IT risk officer. We emphasize that the risk officer manages the process, not the risks, a fact that implies that the risk officer should be a process-oriented manager, not a technical manager with deep expertise in a particular functional risk area.

Figure 5-4 shows the steps in a typical IT risk governance process. The risk governance process is an ongoing cycle with periodic checkpoints, not a one-time effort. Risks evolve over time as the enterprise and its environment changes; risk priorities and policies evolve in response. We discuss each of the process components next.

FIGURE 5-4

Steps in the IT risk governance process

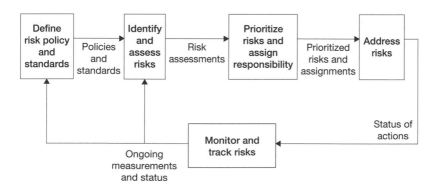

Source: © 2005, Gartner, Inc. Adapted from *Best Practices Council for IT Security Executives Report on IT Security Governance,* December 2005.

Defining Risk Policy and Standards

Policy defines what is, and is not, permissible or required and what actions and activities are necessary to ensure that what is required is done and what is not permissible is prohibited. Standards define how policy is to be implemented. Policies tend to be relatively broader than standards because they are in part statements of principle (e.g., "the security and privacy of personally identifiable information will be protected according to the most stringent requirements of the nations in which we do business" and "information [such as the customer, order, or part] will be recorded once and used in the same way for all business processes"). Standards tend to be specific because they are designed to guide the implementation of processes, procedures, software and hardware configuration, and so on (e.g., "all desktops will use Windows XP Service Pack 2 with the following services disabled" and "we will deploy only the following configurations of desktops and laptops").

Policy or standards may be defined by referring to existing bodies of knowledge (such as model policies and general or industry-specific regulations, like Gramm-Leach-Bliley in financial services and HIPAA in health care), enterprise-specific technical architectures, and so on. Model policies, such as the industry-standard information security policy ISO 17799, tend to be extremely comprehensive and detailed to cover every possible contingency. Enterprises with pressing needs or little patience for detail are best served by selectively implementing subsets or combinations of industry-standard policies focused on the enterprise's most critical vulnerabilities, as discussed in chapter 3.

Identifying and Assessing Risks

Identifying and assessing risks is the core of effective risk management. As PFPC's Michael Harte noted, a risk that is not known cannot be managed. The process of identifying and assessing IT risks is carried out at multiple levels:

- Individual managers and experts first identify and assess risks that exist within their own spheres of control, as well as those risks outside their spheres of control that may impact their responsibilities.

- Groups of managers and experts jointly compare and assess the risks that they have individually identified and assessed to produce a consolidated view of risks at their level of the enterprise.

- In large complex enterprises, risks may be consolidated and compared again at higher levels of the enterprise.

In risk-averse cultures (as described in chapter 6), managers and experts may find it easier to identify risks than to talk about them. One of the roles of an IT risk manager is to help employees involved in a risk discussion speak freely—and free, not to mention frequent, conversations about risk is a critical success factor for effective risk management. Our data shows that enterprises that manage risks effectively conduct identification and assessment exercises an average of four times per year, or almost three times as frequently as less effective enterprises. Most risk-aware enterprises find that key managers spend one half to one full day per quarter identifying and assessing IT risks.

In general, assessing a risk is about defining the risk's potential to cause harm to the enterprise. The relevant questions, therefore, are about likelihood ("how likely is this kind of incident to occur?") and impact ("what harm would occur if this event happened?"). Where IT risk is concerned, the likelihood of an incident can't be assessed adequately without knowledgeable IT personnel. Impact can best be determined by knowledgeable business personnel. Therefore, an assessment process that doesn't include both IT and business personnel is fatally flawed from the start.

It should go without saying that likelihood and impact vary among different businesses—even for the same risks—due to each enterprise's situation, vulnerabilities, and circumstances. In most locations, availability risks from environmental threats—such as earthquakes, fire, floods, or hurricanes—would reasonably be considered high impact but low likelihood. Publicly traded companies facing the need to certify their financials for Sarbanes-Oxley usually consider accuracy risks in financial processes as high impact, with the corresponding likelihood varying with the age and quality of supporting systems and processes.

Some enterprises extend their likelihood/impact assessments by adding factors that are specific to their contexts. Barnardo's, the United Kingdom's largest children's charity, adds a third factor (manager concern), as shown in table 5-1, which is taken from Barnardo's IT risk register.[5] This factor is explicitly intended as a "gut check" to bring a manager's intuitive, emotional response to a risk—something that Barnardo's thinks is dangerous to ignore—into the assessment process.

The likelihood of a specific risk incident is often the hardest number to estimate. Because of the newness and complexity of IT risk, IT risk managers don't have the detailed actuarial information that insurance companies use to price other types of risk. However, nothing so accurate is needed. Although an enterprise may have hundreds of documented IT risks, risk managers can get to the handful that are most important by using templates or other tools to develop broadly consistent assessments without actuarial levels of precision.

In general, simple, clearly defined measures for both likelihood and impact are adequate to focus the enterprise's attention on the risks that matter most. It is often good enough to assess risks in broad categories of impact and likelihood, such as high, medium, and low. That approach makes risk assessment relatively simple and allows the most significant risks to quickly bubble up to the top. Consistency is critical; it is *not* enough to ask people to put a high/medium/low label on impact and likelihood because perceptions of

TABLE 5-1

Top line of Barnardo's 2004 IT risk register

Risk name	Controls	Weaknesses	Action points	Probability	Impact	Concern	Risk factor
Data loss or compromise of IT systems	• Audit trail of changes	• Lack of DPA knowledge	• Train/educate in DPA	2	5	4	40
• Serious Data Protection Act (DPA) leak	• Strong external defense of IT systems		• Increase internal controls (training module to be prepared)				
• Hacking of systems	• Password/access controls						
• Unauthorized access	• Policy on passwords						

Source: Richard Hunter, George Westerman, and Dave Aron, "IT Risk Management: A Little Bit More Is a Whole Lot Better," Research Report (Stamford, CT: Gartner Executive Programs, February 2005).

the meaning and importance of those terms varies from person to person (recall George and Marilyn's different risk priorities on the playground). At a minimum, enterprises should provide guidelines about how to classify impact and likelihood, even when the categories used are apparently intuitive.

The next two figures show examples of simple and more complex assessment mechanisms used by two companies we studied. In figure 5-5, the chemical company mentioned earlier defines a risk as "low impact" if it affects less than 5 percent of working capital (at whatever corporate level it is being examined), "high impact" if it affects more than 10 percent of working capital, and "medium impact" if it falls in between. The company assesses a risk as "high likelihood" if an incident is 50 percent likely within a year, "low likelihood" if it is not likely within five years, and "medium likelihood" if it falls in between. (Please note that, for explanatory purposes only, we superimposed a set of access risks from a large high-tech firm in 2002. Actual risk maps would list risks on all 4A's.)

If more rigorous methods are required, firms can use checklists and diagnostics to standardize the risk assessment process. Note the rating scheme used by TD Banknorth, as depicted in figure 5-6. This ranking scheme is relatively complex, but it's clearly defined and straightforward enough to be applied quickly. While the scheme doesn't yield precise estimates of impact and likelihood, TD Banknorth's risk officer, Tom Prince, believes it accurately identifies the relative levels of impact and likelihood of each risk.[6]

In short, simple approaches to quantifying likelihood and impact produce effective assessments for IT risks. Above all, risk assessment is a prediction, and there's no point in quantifying a prediction to three decimal places when the variables involved are themselves numerous and difficult to quantify accurately.[7]

A recurrent question in assessment is what to do about risks that are extremely unlikely but will have a huge impact should they come to pass—like the collapse of a building, the loss of availability result-

FIGURE 5-5

Risk map showing well-specified broad criteria for assessing impact and likelihood

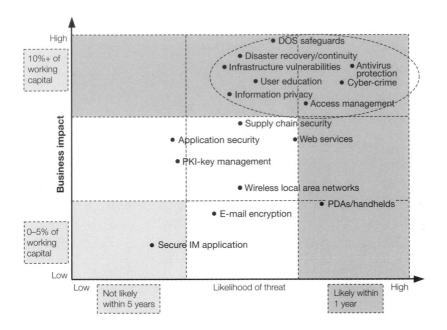

Note: Risks shown are a limited subset from an information security unit. Actual risk maps would have a full set of risks on all four A's.

Source: © 2007 MIT Sloan Center for Information Systems Research. Used with permission.

ing from a chemical spill or flood, or a terrorist attack. Multiplying a likelihood at or near zero by a substantial potential for harm results in an assessment that puts the risk at or near zero on a combined scale. But if the risk is ignored, it may cost the enterprise dearly.

An effective approach to dealing with such very-low-likelihood risks is to eliminate likelihood from the calculation, assess the importance of the risk based on impact, and perform a cost-benefit analysis of options for dealing with it. This approach doesn't make it any easier to know when such risks will occur, if ever, but it does give the enterprise insight into whether there are cost-effective options for prioritizing and handling them.

FIGURE 5-6

IT risk assessment approach based on diagnostic scales

Risk impact category	Rating	Weight	Weighted impact score
Service area impacted	8	1	8
Business function criticality	4	1	4
Customer impact	4	3	12
Financial impact	2	3	6
Data sensitivity	2	2	4
TOTAL (risk IMPACT score)			34

Risk likelihood category	Rating	Weight	Weighted likelihood score
Difficulty of exploit	8	3	24
Number of points of entry	2	2	4
Required location	4	1	4
Detection speed	4	1	4
Response planned	4	3	12
TOTAL (risk LIKELIHOOD score)			48

Measurement	Criterion	Rating
High-criticality functions	Business functions could not be down more than 4 hours.	8
Medium-criticality functions	Business functions could be down more than 4 hours but less than 24 hours.	4
Low-criticality functions	Business functions could be down 24 hours or more.	2

Source: © 2007 MIT Sloan Center for Information Systems Research. Adapted from TD Banknorth documents. Used with permission.

Many enterprises take a final step to test individual managers' assessments against the opinions of their peers, usually via live group discussion. This is a useful way to ensure that assessments are comprehensive and reasonable and, therefore, provide a meaningful basis for decisions.

Prioritizing Risks and Assigning Responsibility

Prioritization and assessment are not the same thing, though risks assessed as having high impact and/or likelihood are in most cases likely to rise to the top of the priority list as well. The nature of a risk—meaning what is actually *at risk*—and the ability of the enterprise to deal with the risk effectively at a reasonable cost can affect its priority, along with other enterprise priorities and constraints. Prioritization is followed by assigning someone responsibility for handling the risk via mitigation, avoidance, acceptance, or transference.

Prioritization must be the responsibility of the relevant level of business management. Responsibility for managing the risk can be delegated; responsibility for prioritization can't be. This is another reason why IT risks must be described in terms of business consequences, ideally beginning with the 4A model.

Addressing Risks

Each risk can be managed in a combination of four ways: reducing, avoiding, transferring (such as through insurance or partnership), or accepting. In most cases, the preferred means of handling an IT risk is to reduce its likelihood (e.g., by improving the foundation) or its impact (e.g., by making plans for manual recovery in a business continuity plan). Many IT risks associated with accuracy are unavoidable as a matter of regulation; risks associated with access are increasingly dangerous, so they cannot be accepted and are difficult to transfer; risks associated with agility can't generally be transferred, but they also can't be accepted or avoided by most enterprises.

As described in the introduction, Comair had no contingency plan for the failure of its crew-scheduling system and so, in effect, accepted a risk with a low probability but a potentially disastrous impact.[8] Given that the potential impact of the scheduling system's failure, no matter the likelihood, was very high, Comair would have been well served by a plan that recognized the impact and described contingencies. In other words, acceptance is only an option when you understand the very worst that can happen and are prepared to live with the consequences, regardless of likelihood.

Our data tells us that focusing on vulnerabilities is more effective in reducing risk than focusing on threats. In fact, of nine specific types of threats we examined in our survey, none proved to be statistically significantly related to increased risk, although many vulnerabilities were. The enterprise can do little at best to control threats, especially external ones, but it can do a lot to control vulnerabilities. Focusing on vulnerabilities reduces an enterprise's tendency to react to what is apparently most urgent—such as the threat reported in yesterday's newspaper—and helps the enterprise act instead to reduce vulnerabilities that might be exploited by any number of threats. No nation can control the level of the sea, but a nation can build dikes to reduce the vulnerability of its lands to high waters; no enterprise can control a sea of external hackers, but an enterprise can plug the holes in its network dike that hackers might otherwise exploit.

In short, vulnerabilities, not threats, are the root cause for high risk exposure, and it's best to focus on the root cause.

Monitoring and Tracking Risks

Monitoring and tracking risks means observing and recording both the effectiveness of risk management plans and policies and the effects of changing internal and external circumstances on risks under management. It also means monitoring key risk indicators that measure conditions that are associated with the 4A's: availability (e.g., the consistency of hardware and software configurations, calls to the help desk, or transaction volumes), access (e.g., employee turnover), accuracy (e.g., timeliness and accuracy of reports), and agility (e.g., percentage of projects completed on time and on budget). Monitoring systems functions can often be done automatically by the systems that support a process; for example, data on how vulnerable an enterprise's network is to attack may be gathered automatically by the software used to repel attacks. But in most enterprises, monitoring includes procedures and processes that are carried out by human beings—teams of technical and business personnel who regularly inspect systems and business processes for vulnerabilities and compliance to policy and standards.

TeliaSonera, the leading telecommunications company in the Nordic and Baltic regions, rotates monthly application security reviews among business units for all existing processes and supporting systems and for all systems under development.[9] Each review is planned and approved by the IT Security Council (the implementation council in the IT risk governance structure) and announced well in advance, along with the questions that will used in the review and the people who will be interviewed. The review leader selects the members of the review team, which always includes a representative of the business unit that owns the application or process to be inspected.[10]

TeliaSonera's reviews are aimed at cooperation and awareness rather than finding fault. "We give best-practice recommendations, which [the business units] can follow or not," says Toni Bekker, TeliaSonera's corporate senior manager for IT risk. "Our best practices often come from where we find excellence, which we then propagate through the company. When we do find fault, we agree with the owner about the time needed to correct it. Things are always right the second time."[11]

Figure 5-7 shows the structure of a review process such as Telia-Sonera's. A "trigger event" is anything that would cause the risk team to initiate a review. This includes events such as a key risk indicator reaching a warning level, a regularly (or randomly) scheduled review of a system, due diligence for a potential acquisition, investigating a new partner or vendor (or verifying an existing one), a "gate" review of an application currently in development, or anything else that suggests the firm should examine vulnerabilities, verify compliance, or reassess risk.

What an enterprise chooses to monitor in greatest detail *first* depends heavily on its assessments of risk. Ideally, enterprises would track the impact of every system outage, every hacker break-in, every instance of loss due to inaccurate data, every employee who quits her job, and any other incident (such as the completion or cancellation of a project) that has risk consequences. At the start, to focus effort and energy where they matter most, it's more useful to develop metrics for the highest-priority risks, to tie those metrics directly to business performance (e.g., call center uptime, as opposed to network up-

FIGURE 5-7

Steps in a typical risk review process

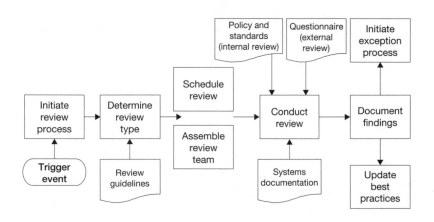

Source: © 2007 Gartner, Inc., and MIT Sloan Center for Information Systems Research. Used with permission.

time), and to expand the set of metrics as those risks are brought under better control. In time, instead of repeatedly conducting detailed assessments of all risks, firms can shift to incrementally updating status on existing risks coupled with targeted new risk assessments.

PFPC, for example, monitors turnover of IT employees. If it is too low, IT executives assess whether they should encourage more people to leave. If turnover exceeds a critical threshold, they assess how to change policies or pay rates to avoid losing key skills. PFPC also tracks the overall skills base of its IT employees to ensure that it hires the right skills for the future and doesn't lose skills that are critical for keeping the business running right now. Because availability is critical to PFPC's value proposition, the company also tracks the performance of its infrastructure, high-severity calls to the help desk, and the performance of each application development vendor. None are perfect indicators of risk, but together they can highlight particular assets, projects, or business units in which risk is increasing. Figure 5-8 shows an example of the IT risk monitoring and reporting dashboard used by PFPC.

In addition to improving the process of assessing and prioritizing risks, monitoring provides important feedback on the effectiveness of policy and standards. If monitoring finds that certain policies or standards are frequently violated, it may be the policy or standard—not the behavior of the business units or IT staff—that's the problem.

Five Key Practices of an Effective IT Risk Governance Process

Our survey analysis identifies five practices enterprises can use to improve their risk governance processes. Enterprises using each of these practices reported statistically significantly higher levels of confidence in their risk management capabilities and less likelihood

FIGURE 5-8

PFPC's IT risk dashboard

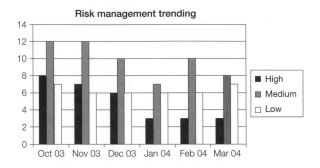

Risk management trending

Risks by rating		Rating		
# of open issues	Total	High	Medium	Low
Beginning of month	19	3	10	6
New risks	3	1	0	2
Closed risks	4	1	2	1
Improved risk rating	0	0	0	0
Declined risk rating	0	0	0	0
End of month	18	3	8	7

	Risk category	Owner	Total	Under 1	1–2	2–3	3–6	6–9	9–12	Over 12
							Months			
Risk aging	Architecture	Manager A	2					1	1	
	Financial control	Manager B	2		1			1		
	Human capital	Manager C	1				1			
	Operations	Manager D	6		2			1	3	
	Project mgmt.	Manager E	1		1					
	Security	Manager F	6	2	1			1	2	
	Strategy	Manager G	0							
		Total	18	2	5	0	1	4	6	0

Source: George Westerman and Robert Walpole, "PFPC: Building and IT Risk Management Competency," working paper 352, Center for Information Systems Research, MIT Sloan School of Management, Cambridge, MA. Used with permission.

Note: Managers' names removed to protect confidentiality.

that they were unaware of important risks. These risk governance practices do not cost much more than haphazard ones, and they ensure consistency in the process, accountability to manage and monitor the process, and a mechanism to improve the process over time. Some of these five practices have already been described; we list them here to emphasize their importance.

1. *Appoint a single person to be in charge of the process.* As leader of the IT risk management team, the IT risk officer designs and runs the risk management process—setting policy, identifying risk, prioritizing risk, managing risk, and tracking risk—but does not manage particular risks. By making a single person accountable for the process, effective enterprises gain a clear focus on IT risk management and a mechanism for continuous improvement.

2. *Identify formal risk categories.* A small but comprehensive set of well-defined categories for IT risks and risk factors improves the risk management process in two ways. First, the categories and their definitions serve as a checklist to help local experts identify and assess risks. Second, they help higher levels of the organization prioritize and monitor risks by grouping similar risks across the enterprise; this is a useful step before comparing risks across categories. We recommend using the 4A's as a basis for high-level categorization. Some enterprises may add one or more categories, if needed, for their particular circumstances.

3. *Create a risk register.* An IT risk register records and tracks all IT risks. At a minimum, the risk register identifies the risk's name, description, category, and owner, as well as the risk's potential impact and likelihood. The register also tracks any action planned for dealing with the risk and whether progress is being made. Some enterprises also

track additional data elements that include the IT resources, business processes, and organizational units
affected by the risk; the expected date of resolution; and
the current status. Companies can use expensive tools that
are dedicated to tracking this information, but they're far
from mandatory. We have seen tools as simple as spreadsheets and word processors used for the process, at least in
the initial stages. What's important is to be able to track
risks at the right levels of detail and to compare all risks,
or certain types of risks, within an organizational unit or
across the enterprise. Table 5-2 shows an excerpt from the
network communications section of PFPC's IT risk register.

4. *Develop consistent methods to assess risk.* Consistent, quan-
tified assessments of risk impact and likelihood improve
the firm's ability to compare and prioritize risks in a global
manner. We discussed this practice in detail earlier in this
chapter; we only wish to emphasize here that a consistent
approach using broad but clearly defined criteria is sufficient to reveal the risks that matter most.

5. *Use specialized best practices.* Industry and vendor best
practices—such as recommended software configurations,
daily virus updates, and standard internal controls—are often
available from industry specialists and trade associations.
Such practices enable risk managers to reliably implement a
baseline of "good enough" risk protection in standard areas,
eliminating vulnerabilities that would otherwise create a high
background level of risk. Risk managers can then focus on
unique circumstances that need special attention.

Our data tells us that these five practices have statistically significant impacts on every category of risk, almost across the board.
Our survey data shows that a third to a half of enterprises have *not*

TABLE 5-2

Excerpt from PFPC's IT risk register

Risk issue	Risk description	Risk type	Risk owner	Rank	Project status	Target date	Project number	Project manager	Comments
Call recorder performance issues at 103 and 400 Bellevue	Performance issues with current Verint and NiceLogger systems affecting 2 LOBs (i.e., lost recordings)	Performance	Manager A	High	Not started	TBD	TBD	TBD	• NWS has submitted proposals for system upgrades to the (2) LOBs • Waiting for LOB decision
Encryption on WAN circuits at Lynnfield	Current encryption on Lynnfield to Summit WAN circuits does not meet PNC standards for 3DES	Security	Manager B	High	Not started	TBD	TBD	TBD	• Related to risk item #3: EOL networking equipment at Lynnfield • Waiting for LOB decision to remediate

Source: George Westerman and Robert Walpole, "PFPC: Building and IT Risk Management Competency," working paper 352, Center for Information Systems Research, MIT Sloan School of Management, Cambridge, MA. Used with permission.

FIGURE 5-9

Adoption of key practices for the IT risk governance process

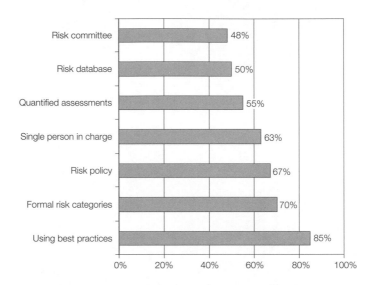

Source: @ 2007 MIT Sloan Center for Information Systems Research. Used with permission.

Note: Bars represent percentage of surveyed organizations stating that they use a practice consistently.

implemented at least one of these best practices—so there's plenty of room for improvement in many enterprises. (See figure 5-9 for the prevalence of certain practices.) We should emphasize here that these practices cannot substitute for a well-managed risk governance process; they can only improve one that already exists. A robust process is essential to focus managerial attention and organizational awareness on IT risk and to ensure that the firm is taking action to address the most important risks.

Implementing the IT Risk Governance Process at PFPC

PFPC's experience introducing IT risk governance shows both the value and the effort involved in adopting new IT risk governance processes. It took leadership from CIO Michael Harte and other IT managers to inculcate the process in their units and with their business counterparts, and it required senior executives of the business units to encourage their people to participate in IT risk management processes and reviews as needed.[12]

To start the process, PFPC's IT risk officer adapted enterprise risk management processes from its parent company, PNC Financial. The process required that each of the CIO's seven deputies identify risks in their areas and across the firm's business units. These risks were recorded in a risk register (an excerpt of which is shown in table 5-2), from which the risk officer compiled reports for Harte, the Technology Risk Management Council, and the firm's Enterprise Risk Committee.

The process did not run smoothly at the start. The first iteration identified more than three hundred risks. As one IT executive said, "There's too much detail. We're overwhelming Michael Harte, and as a result, he goes into the corporate risk meetings feeling like he's not adequately prepared to fight for a few key risks." There were also issues in consistency and motives, leading some IT managers to identify very few risks, while others identified dozens.

As it turns out, some people were reluctant to lists their risks, since they considered risk management to be part of their responsibilities; reporting a risk that a manager could resolve himself seemed to be troubling the CIO with information he did not need to worry about. Others chose to use the risk management process to replace detailed issue lists required for project management or vendor management. Still others appeared to use the risk identification exercise for political purposes; a manager might try to improve his image by reporting few risks in his area or to tarnish the image of a vendor or another unit by reporting many risks relating to that vendor's or unit's area.

Over time, Harte's senior staff developed consistent definitions of high, medium, and low risks and consolidated risks that occurred across multiple applications or business units. They also improved governance processes to identify risks early and to encourage alternative lower-risk approaches in technology decisions.

In addition to improving assessment consistency and prioritization of risks, PFPC's IT managers also improved identification and monitoring. Each month, the IT risk officer asked IT leaders to refresh their risk status and then ran updated status reports (such as those shown in figure 5-8). Harte reviewed these reports in his senior staff meeting to ensure that he knew about the most important risks and that his staff was focused on reducing them. The IT unit also began to monitor key risk indicators, such as staff turnover and calls to the help desk, as early warning signals of potential risks. The IT team began to make proactive efforts to improve areas, such as personnel skills and vendor management, that had the potential to become serious availability, access, accuracy, or agility risks in the future.

As the IT risk governance processes matured, PFPC began to embed risk management into all the firm's IT management processes. For example, the company added steps to the new project approval process to identify potential operational risks and project delivery risks (see areas enclosed in dotted lines in figure 5-10). Projects that did not follow enterprise standards or that might require extra support in the data center were identified early, and project sponsors were encouraged to modify their plans to reduce risk.

Embedding risk management into IT management processes had numerous benefits. Encouraging managers to use standards and to choose low-risk technical decisions prevented new IT projects from inadvertently worsening the firm's risk profile. Identifying exceptions early prepared the firm for nonstandard projects and encouraged managers to consider whether policy should change. Making managers think about all aspects of risk when requesting new projects created awareness among project sponsors of the conditions that produce high risk. And knowing about projects that would affect a particular IT asset enabled architecture managers to piggyback on existing projects to gradually simplify the foundation.

FIGURE 5-10

Risk management incorporated into PFPC's IT demand management

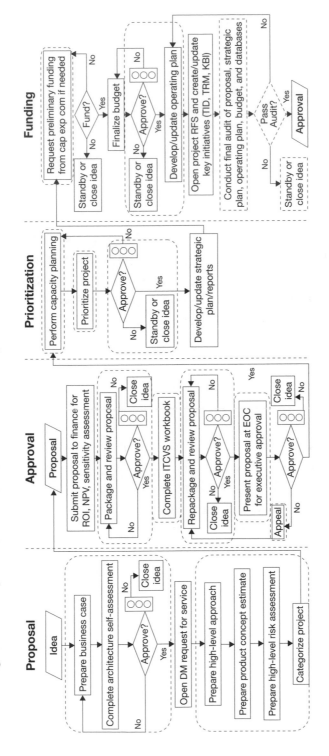

Source: George Westerman and Robert Walpole, "PFPC: Building and IT Risk Management Competency," working paper 352, Center for Information Systems Research, MIT Sloan School of Management, Cambridge, MA. Used with permission.

Within fifteen months, the number of active risks had been reduced tenfold, Harte and his staff had a clear focus on the risks that were most important to the enterprise, and the firm had passed its first-ever IT-specific audit by the Federal Reserve. IT risk management was becoming an established part of doing business, rather than an additional bureaucratic responsibility. Business executives and their IT counterparts began to understand that standards and governance processes not only reduced risk but also improved the effectiveness of the firm's IT organization and assets—in other words, they started to see the business value of IT risk management.

A clear sign of business appreciation for the value of IT risk management arrived when the sales organization began taking Harte on calls to showcase the firm's IT risk management capabilities to prospects. Not all CIOs can expect similar customer attention for their IT risk management processes, but other benefits, stated earlier, are clear.

Process is essential to gaining focus on the IT risks that matter most. Awareness and a solid foundation by themselves can't create the necessary understanding to guide executive decisions. Without process, there's no way to bring people throughout the enterprise together, again and again, to find out what the risk elephant really looks like as conditions change and the enterprise's risk profile changes with them. Although the rigor and bureaucratic weight of the process may differ between enterprises, all need a competent process that tailors the practices listed in this chapter to the context of the enterprise.

Our next chapter describes the third risk management discipline: risk awareness.

Six

Building a Risk-Aware Culture

NOT TOO LONG AGO, Richard visited Chevron Phillips Chemical's offices in Houston, Texas. He heard his first company message about safety when he pulled up to the entrance of the parking lot and was informed by a security officer that the speed limit was 9.5 miles per hour. The officer further told Richard to "please be safe." Richard saw two safety-related posters before he passed the front desk and more on the walls everywhere he went.

Richard commented on the safety-related messages to his host, who confirmed that safety was indeed a priority at Chevron Phillips Chemical. Richard was told that there was a safety theme every month, and employees routinely received all sorts of information, in formats ranging from live discussions to memos and e-mails, about how to handle the safety risks associated with the theme.

"What's the theme this month?" Richard asked.

"Watch out for venomous snakes," his host said.

The culture at Chevron Phillips Chemical is obviously oriented to safety. There are good reasons why this is so. The materials the employees handle are volatile and dangerous, and a mistake or an accident might do a lot of harm quickly. And beyond all that, there are venomous snakes in the neighborhood.

It's important to know about such risks and to spread the knowledge. People who don't know a threat or vulnerability when they see one can't be expected to protect themselves or their enterprise. ChipCo (as described in chapter 3) has a beautifully well-structured and secure IT foundation. But that did not stop a manufacturing engineer from potentially jeopardizing ChipCo's network when he installed a wireless card in his desktop PC in contravention of the company's security policies, inadvertently providing a way hackers could access the company's network from the plant's parking lot. The Pew Internet & American Life Project reported in February 2005 that in the preceding twelve months, 35 percent of online Americans had received a "phishing" attack via e-mail; Pew further estimated that 2 percent of online Americans, unaware of the dangers of phishing or of how to spot a phishing scam, had unwittingly responded to such dangerous e-mails.[1]

Lack of risk awareness opens leaks throughout the foundation and cripples the effectiveness of the risk governance process. Without awareness, enterprises can't avoid risks; they can only suffer the consequences. But a risk-aware culture is not merely a culture that possesses widespread knowledge of risks and solutions. A risk-aware culture has certain distinct characteristics, starting with a high degree of "psychological safety"—the freedom to discuss things without the fear of retribution—when discussing risks is concerned.[2] When a culture is risk aware, people know their risks, are comfortable discussing their risks with others, and are willing to help others resolve risks. People in such a culture have the ability to face and learn from managed failures (as opposed to careless failures), which improves performance over time, and to share risks and deal with them as a team.

A Risk-Averse Culture Is Far from Risk-Free

A risk-averse culture is one in which individuals have a low degree of psychological safety where risk management is concerned. To be precise, they are afraid, not just of risks, but of others' disapproval or censure where risks are concerned. In a risk-averse culture, people automatically avoid taking actions that might produce risk, without asking whether the risks can be controlled or are worth the potential rewards. Failure and risky behavior are publicly punished as an example to others (see figure 6-1).

A risk-averse culture doesn't really avoid risk: it avoids discussion of risk, consciousness of risk, and understanding of risk. Risk is always present, whether it's acknowledged or not, but a risk-averse culture refuses to face up to it. The same kinds of failures happen over and over because there's no opportunity to capture the learning

FIGURE 6-1

Risk-averse and risk-aware cultures

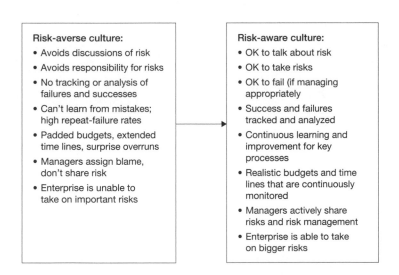

Risk-averse culture:
- Avoids discussions of risk
- Avoids responsibility for risks
- No tracking or analysis of failures and successes
- Can't learn from mistakes; high repeat-failure rates
- Padded budgets, extended time lines, surprise overruns
- Managers assign blame, don't share risk
- Enterprise is unable to take on important risks

Risk-aware culture:
- OK to talk about risk
- OK to take risks
- OK to fail (if managing appropriately
- Success and failures tracked and analyzed
- Continuous learning and improvement for key processes
- Realistic budgets and time lines that are continuously monitored
- Managers actively share risks and risk management
- Enterprise is able to take on bigger risks

Source: © 2007 MIT Sloan Center for Information Systems Research and Gartner, Inc. Used with permission.

that goes with failure. Instead of creating solutions for risky situations, people avoid responsibility and seek scapegoats. In this culture risk avoidance isn't a choice or a strategy. It's a reflex.

A Risk-Aware Culture Starts at the Top

Organizational cultures don't change from risk averse to risk aware on their own. Experts in organizational change management generally agree that senior executives, by their words and deeds, define the dominant culture of the enterprise. Executives who want to create a risk-aware enterprise will be faced with hard decisions, and they need to think through their responses in advance. For example:

- Will senior executives actively encourage business unit managers to use new organizational mechanisms to examine IT risks in their established and new products and services—even if new or existing products must be revised as a result? Microsoft did exactly that with its Trustworthy Computing initiative, as described in chapter 8. ChoicePoint implemented new mechanisms for this purpose in the wake of its highly publicized loss of more than one hundred fifty thousand personal records in February 2005.[3]

- What principles will executives apply when resolving exceptions to policy? For example, if a manager skirts IT governance processes and reviews to get a system—and the new product or relationships the system supports—implemented faster, how will executives handle the situation and the precedents it may set?

- How will executives treat proposals for initiatives that involve nonstandard technologies that will result in a more complex foundation?

- How will executives treat people who report risks and ask for help in mitigating those risks? How will they treat subordinates who take intelligent risks and fail?

- How will executives get and use information that will help the company assess and manage risks?

- How will executives deal with a manager of a risky project who manages competently but still is not able to bring the project in on time?

- How will executives treat project managers who slow a project down to deal with risks that have suddenly appeared, such as the loss or reassignment of the project sponsor?

The trade-offs involved in questions such as these are not trivial. The ways that executives respond to such questions send important signals to everyone in the enterprise about which risks matter and how much they matter.

As an example of the important role of senior executives in changing the risk culture, consider Celanese Chemical, a $6 billion global manufacturer of acetyl products and engineered polymers.[4] Prior to spinning off from global chemical giant Hoechst, Celanese was a company in which "nothing ever failed." Employees always played it safe; they underpromised and overbudgeted, and management was tolerant. But the new company's debt load made dramatic improvements in performance necessary, which in turn demanded a new culture with a much higher tolerance for risk. According to CIO Karl Wachs, "At the time we spun off from Hoechst, we had about $2 billion [of] debt. We couldn't operate in a conventional way. In a conventional way, we would still be at the same position, maybe 5–10 percent better. We had to get the company to the next level."

Part of the transformation was "One SAP," a radical consolidation of seven ERP systems (and all the variations in business process that implies) to one. The change to a risk-aware culture began with

Wachs's first presentation of the project to the board, in which he gave an honest estimate of price and schedule—without the 100 percent or more padding that was normal for project proposals at Celanese. He further informed the board that because the estimate had no excess slack, the "never fail" guarantees that were traditional for the company did not apply. The board considered this ambitious, nontraditional proposal and decided that the project was a go, not only to implement the transformation of company processes, but to introduce a new attitude toward risk.

According to Wachs, "Risk taking is a good thing. If you don't take risks, you never go to greatness. You shouldn't make stupid mistakes. But if you make mistakes or things go wrong, be able to stand up and say 'something is wrong here' so the team can fix it." These are simple words, but consider the dramatic change they represent for a culture in which previously "nothing ever failed."

With the project approved, Wachs took steps to help his team develop the right risk-aware culture. He picked team leaders who would be comfortable with open discussions of status and risk. Then he and his team worked to model the right behaviors and instill the culture throughout the team conducting this massive project.

Wachs explained, "When you have a multiyear, hundred-people project, things go wrong. On a day-to-day basis, things change. What you have to do is create an atmosphere where change is normal, where people understand that you take a risk, and if things change, or if you're not ready, you say so, and then you adapt your plan and move on. What's key for that is honest communication."

The One SAP plan needed constant adjustment to keep up with changes in the company. According to Wachs:

> Throughout the project, we had issues. We bought companies, we sold companies, the various divisions decided to add things, and so on. And every day in the project, it looks as if this is a disaster. Every morning something doesn't work. And you always have to manage your reserves. And you have to understand when you approach the critical line.

In the summer of 2003, we approached the critical line. As soon as we knew we couldn't make the date in a quality way, we immediately went to the board and said, "We have a problem. We need three more months."

It was interesting . . . to see how the organization reacted. The people on the team were actually skeptical that people would survive this thing because it wasn't just about the three months. It was about money, a serious amount of money.

We went to the board and clearly explained, from a very factual base, where we were, why we were there, and what to do next. And they fully supported us. They immediately published a blurb on the intranet saying that "the Board fully accepts that we want to delay this thing because we want to deliver a quality system." They positively supported that kind of culture. And that really helped the organization dramatically in understanding that taking risk is okay.

Wachs had been straightforward with the board all along, and the board members reciprocated. They had seen the project team encounter and overcome earlier risks, and they knew by now that they could rely on what they were hearing. In turn, they did their part to encourage the transformation of the culture by offering help to the project team instead of punishing the team for slipping the schedule. Most important, board members proved with their decision that the board was now willing to take calculated risks, too.

To Improve Awareness, Segment the Audience and Communicate Frequently

Improving awareness requires more than just modeling and rewarding risk-aware behaviors. Our data shows a strong link between awareness training and overall risk reduction. As shown in figure 6-2, in a group of general mechanisms (e.g., those not focused specifically on one of the 4A's), it is the only mechanism statistically significantly correlated with lower risk on all 4A's.

FIGURE 6-2

The effectiveness of awareness training

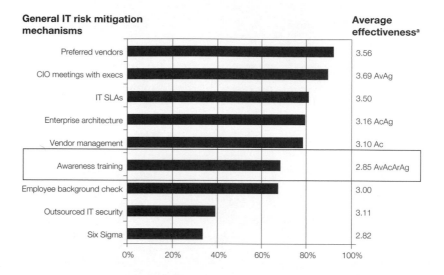

General IT risk mitigation mechanisms / **Average effectiveness**[a]

Mechanism	Effectiveness
Preferred vendors	3.56
CIO meetings with execs	3.69 AvAg
IT SLAs	3.50
Enterprise architecture	3.16 AcAg
Vendor management	3.10 Ac
Awareness training	2.85 AvAcArAg
Employee background check	3.00
Outsourced IT security	3.11
Six Sigma	2.82

Source: © 2007 MIT Sloan Center for Information Systems Research. Used with permission.

[a]Average effectiveness scores are on a scale of 1 (ineffective) to 5 (highly effective) as rated by 119 survey respondents. The letters *Av, Ac, Ar,* and *Ag* indicate that using the mechanism was associated with statistically significantly more risk mitigation for availability, access, accuracy, and agility change, respectively.

Risk is a complex topic, and it is not feasible or effective for everyone to understand all of it. Specialists need to understand lots of details, but most people only need to understand risk in terms of what creates risk for them and what they can do to reduce their vulnerability to those risks.

Table 6-1 includes excerpts from a presentation by the IT risk officer for ING Insurance Americas that describe plans to increase IT risk awareness among ING employees and customers. While culture is firmly in the hands of senior management, it is typical for awareness plans to be the responsibility of the corporate or IT risk officer or, in a smaller organization, the head of information security.

Note that this plan describes various audiences and their goals. Not shown on these charts is that the funds allocated for customer awareness are significantly greater than those allocated for internal awareness, in keeping with the IT risk management program's theme: "making it easier to do business with ING in a secure way." Finally, note that the value proposition for the program includes benefits for both customers and the company.

In general, the audiences for enterprise IT risk awareness communications include executives, managers at the business unit level, end users, IT staff, and external parties such as suppliers and customers. To some extent, these audiences overlap. All employees are technology users in addition to their more specific roles and so must be informed of issues and answers that affect all employees. Awareness includes

TABLE 6-1

ING Insurance Americas' risk awareness goals for information security

ING employee information security awareness program (internal focus)

Definition	The security awareness program is an ongoing communication and education campaign to help users understand their role in protecting ING and customer information and further embed information security into our culture. The goal is to inform users that they are accountable for ensuring the integrity, confidentiality, privacy, and availability of information assets. The program reaches approximately 26,000 ING employees across Canada, Latin America, and the United States. Additional targeted audiences include executives, people managers, new employees, information asset owners, information technology staff, third parties (where appropriate), and brokers.
Value proposition	• Become a risk-aware organization • Meet compliance and regulatory requirements
Associated risk	• Inadequate people-risk awareness • Indirectly supports the top 10 risks

2006 activity	• Continue to deploy Insurance Americas information security awareness program with other risk management functions:
	  • Upgrade all employee training programs (in progress)
	  • IRM newsletter (ongoing)
	  • Refinement of training program and employee communications based on employee feedback
	  • Additional training for targeted audiences
	  • Implementation of ING Group's Information Security Knowledge Zone (in progress)
	  • Monthly online articles (ongoing)
	  • Annual security awareness week (ongoing)

(continued)

TABLE 6-1 *(continued)*

ING customer awareness program (external focus)

Definition	The customer awareness program helps ING customers protect themselves against fraud and identity theft. Project scope: • Legal considerations and strategy • Customer-facing considerations and strategy • Technology considerations and strategy
Value proposition	• Minimize brand, reputation, and financial risks associated with identity theft • Reduce ING legal liability • Meet compliance and regulatory requirements
Associated risk	• Unauthorized access • Insecure systems design and change management

2006 activity	• Jointly implement Insurance Americas' anti-phishing strategy and customer campaign with other risk management functions (e.g., ORM, compliance, legal, and CAS)
	• Anti-phishing workgroup is established to:
	  • Create an overall anti-phishing strategy
	  • Involve legal to ensure that all Web sites have an appropriate legal statement to protect ING
	  • Develop and deploy an education campaign for ING customers and clients
	  • Partner with other ING business units globally to leverage knowledge and better coordinate communication and incident response

Source: Materials and background provided by Hsiao-Wei Tang, IT risk officer, ING Americas, 2005. Used with permission.

knowing information such as what the company's IT risk policies are and how to comply with them; how to recognize when colleagues or contractors are engaged in dangerous behavior; what actions to take when a risky situation is identified; and how to recognize threats (such as phishing, spoofing, or virus attacks) in the environment.

To a large extent, many of the issues and messages that apply to internal users—such as how to recognize a threat and what to do when a threat appears—apply to external customers as well. The difference is that the company has less control over how its customers behave and, therefore, must rely more on education and persuasion and less on formal training and enforcement.

As of this writing, no companies that we know of, other than Internet service providers such as AOL and EarthLink, have taken explicit responsibility for protecting their customers from IT risks such as spam and viruses. But many companies, including Internet-based retailers and financial services providers, have taken steps to educate their customers about the risks of Internet-based attacks. Visitors to eBay who click on "Help" from the main page immediately see a list of "Top Questions About eBay." The first item in that list is "How do I know an e-mail is really from eBay?" Another section on the page is headed "Online Security" and includes links titled "Identifying Spoof (Fake) E-mail," "Protecting Yourself from Identity Theft," and "More." Clicking on "More" brings up an entire page devoted to online security, beginning with "Top Questions About Online Security." The company obviously knows its customers are interested in this topic and has made it very easy for customers to find a lot of useful information.

As IT-enabled connections between businesses, their customers, and other external communities increase in depth and breadth, businesses need to frequently consider how their role in reducing IT risk for those parties might change.

Finally, all of these audiences are contributors as well as targets for communications about IT risk. For executives and managers, the IT risk governance process offers opportunities for communications about priorities, status, and the effectiveness of policies and procedures; it also helps them learn about risk-aware thinking by simply trying to do it. For employees in general, the IT risk officer can establish formal channels through which employees can quickly report a dangerous situation or a risk incident. For customers, established customer service channels can be used to forward information about IT risks to the IT risk officer.

The most specific audiences include executives, managers, and IT staff. We discuss each of these briefly below.

Awareness for Executives Is About Leadership and Program Status

Executives need to be aware of the potential effect of specific risks on the enterprise's goals, described in terms of business impact, according to the 4A's, for their particular parts of the business. They need to know the progress of ongoing risk management efforts; this includes quantitative and qualitative metrics describing trends in the overall IT risk portfolio, with a focus on the half dozen or so most critical IT risks. They need to understand the structure and function of IT risk governance processes in the enterprise—particularly because the ability of executives to articulate such arrangements is a critical indicator for risk governance success. Finally, they need to understand the duties of sponsorship, such as the importance of participating in risk governance councils, the importance of formally resolving exceptions to policy, and the implications of decisions to make exceptions to policy.

In his regular meetings with senior business executives, Biogen Idec CIO Patrick Purcell uses some of the time to raise awareness about IT risk and the firm's IT risk management activities. Customizing the message helps executives internalize the concepts. According to Purcell:

> When I speak with the business about risk, I speak about the risk area that is of most concern to that part of the organization. So if I'm talking about risk in the finance area, I would talk in terms of Sarbanes-Oxley and the control risk that we might have in that regard . . . Similarly, in a commercial area, you speak about data privacy risk. So in speaking about risk with any given function, you tend to talk about it in light of the key risk points that that function is trying to manage.
>
> But what I also try to do is . . . to communicate across functions to give them an appreciation that we have to have a single IT approach to managing all these risks and that a single set of business

processes and systems has to suffice to address the needs of all of these regulatory environments.[5]

Awareness for Managers Is About Integration and Execution

Improving awareness for midlevel business managers often comes through communications from the executive team, risk policy council, or the enterprise or IT risk officer. Such communications are intended to encourage managers to integrate risk management into everyday business practices and promote a risk-aware culture in their units. Communications to this audience address the managers' role in following IT risk management policies; their role in IT risk governance councils or in business continuity management; and their responsibilities in risk identification and assessment exercises, such as providing input into vulnerabilities and consequences. Finally, managers need to know the most important risks facing their business unit and the enterprise, how each risk is being addressed, the trends in the enterprise's general risk profile and the trends of specific critical risks. One of the best ways of increasing the awareness of midlevel managers is allowing them to learn by doing—in other words, they can learn by participating in well-designed risk governance processes.

Awareness for IT Staff Is About Building Systems in a Risk-Aware Way

IT systems that are poorly designed and managed create risk; IT systems that are well designed and managed detect and reduce risk. Messages to IT staff are aimed at helping them understand how their activities increase or reduce risk, what risk policies and procedures they need to address and how they should address them, and the ways internal IT experts can help make IT systems as risk-free as possible. Awareness for IT staff includes:

- Following IT risk management policies—for example, policies aimed at maintaining adequate documentation for system functions and behavior—and encouraging colleagues to do the same

- Identifying standard organizational practices—such as resource sharing, project management procedures, or how information is used—that unwittingly create risk and working to resolve those practices

- Recognizing when colleagues are engaging in risky behavior and notifying the IT risk officer immediately (see "Insiders Are a Problem and a Solution")

- Assisting implementation-focused risk governance councils when asked to do so and using such councils to provide ongoing feedback on the effectiveness of policies

Insiders Are a Problem and a Solution

The U.S. Secret Service and Computer Emergency Response Team's 2005 report on insider cyber-sabotage found that about a third of those employees who committed sabotage announced their intentions to colleagues before committing the act. About 12 percent of those saboteurs who were caught, before or after committing the act, were turned in by coworkers. In other words, alert employees are an important line of defense.[a]

a. Carnegie Mellon University Software Engineering Institute, "Insider Threat Study: Computer System Sabotage in Critical Infrastructure Sectors" (Pittsburgh: Carnegie Mellon University Software Engineering Institute, May 2005).

- Understanding the most important risks facing the business unit and the enterprise and the means chosen to reduce, transfer, avoid, or accept those risks

- Participating in IT risk identification and assessment exercises by providing input about particular systems' vulnerabilities and the potential consequences of failing to mitigate them

- Providing support and expertise for risk reviews of IT systems

Regular communications are effective ways to raise awareness with IT staff, just as they are for managers. But often more important is the learning-while-doing gained when participating in well-structured IT risk governance processes.

Drive from the Top Down—Persistently

Awareness programs work with senior executive support and the risk governance process to improve the culture—*over time*. Our research shows that it takes most enterprises twelve to eighteen months to reach a baseline level of effectiveness (including awareness) with IT risk management—that is, it takes twelve to eighteen months to get to the point where managers have internalized risk management processes, are executing them competently and efficiently, and are producing assessments of risk that are broadly comparable across business units and risk categories.

In organizations that have a history of risk aversion, managers have learned not to talk about their risks. In these cases it's particularly important that executives provide steady reinforcement to change the culture. The experience of BOC Gases, a U.K.-based energy company that's now a subsidiary of the Linde Group, in reducing project-related risks (and later all IT risks) illustrates the value of leadership and process in changing the risk culture.[6]

BOC's management became more cognizant of risk following a hostile takeover attempt in 2000. By 2001, risk management efforts were under way throughout the company. A full-time IT manager, Janet Nudds, was assigned to the company's risk management department to develop a framework for assessing and mitigating project risk and to ensure adherence to that framework. The framework encompassed project risk (the risk that the project would fail to deliver required functionality on time and on budget); strategic risk (the risk that the project would imperil one or more strategic objectives); operational risk (the risk that the project would not result in a functional operational environment); and deployment risk (the risk that the project would not be deployed properly and on time).[7]

By 2003, the culture was experiencing wider waves of change. A corporate code of conduct governing the social and ethical responsibilities of BOC Group, BOC Gases' parent company at the time, was issued and implemented. BOC Group's chief executive included a statement in the 2003 annual report that read: "I make no apologies for stating that safety remains our highest priority . . . We are concentrating on changing the behavior of everyone in BOC to make sure that safety really does come first."[8] Sensitivity to risk was increasing.

For its part, IT management focused on promoting an important message: project managers who talked about risks got help quickly. Managers who talked about risks were not punished. Instead they got help quickly. By late 2003, the new focus on risk awareness began to pay off. Although project leaders had previously been unwilling to discuss risk for fear of slowing things down, they now actively sought out Janet Nudds when they perceived trouble. "Our culture is changing," Nudds told us. "Just a few years ago, no one would expose a project in trouble. They'd call me up and hope I'd do it for them in my capacity as group IM [information management] audit manager! Now risks are exposed up front."

As managers at BOC Gases generally perceived improved project success rates, the IT risk management framework expanded. By 2004, the company's risk portfolio included about two hundred major IT risks, of which ten were prioritized for action. Country managers were assigned for each of the top ten risks. Audits were conducted in each country, and when a unit failed, the issue was elevated up the management chain and ultimately reached the CIO. Project risk reviews were expanded to include security and business continuity reviews. Within a few years, with management support, risk emerged from the shadows at BOC to become a focal topic for open discussion—and active management.

Don't Wait to Be Hit by a Falling Piano to Become Risk Aware

We like to joke that there are three kinds of executives when IT risk awareness is concerned:

1. There are executives who've been hit by a falling piano and know that falling pianos are dangerous.

2. There are executives who've seen someone else get hit by a falling piano and know that falling pianos are dangerous.

3. There are executives who every day, on their way to work, walk past a dozen unfortunate people who have obviously been crushed by falling pianos—but have not yet realized that falling pianos are dangerous.

(One of our clients recently advised us to add a fourth category: the executive who asks "What's a piano?")

If you're the third (or fourth) kind of executive, we hope that our discussion of IT risk to this point has helped convince you that it's better to become the second kind before you become the first. A risk-aware culture is impossible if executives don't make a point of taking risk seriously, and that means more than attacking risk (or the one who reported it) wherever it appears. It requires leaders who encourage everyone in the business to understand that it is their personal responsibility to know what risk looks like, who assist in helping others deal effectively with risk, and who model, through their own behaviors, that risk management is every person's responsibility.

In other words, it's not fear that defines a risk-aware culture. It's openness. That openness, when combined with the other two risk disciplines, allows the enterprise to take on more risk (and the returns that come with it) without becoming more risky.

With this chapter, we conclude our review of the three basic disciplines of IT risk management. In the next chapter, we'll discuss what it means to be capable in each of the three disciplines and how to choose which focal discipline should be the rallying point for risk management in your organization.

In the meantime, please be safe—and watch out for falling pianos and venomous snakes.

Seven

Bringing the Three Disciplines Up to Speed

I T'S IMPORTANT for every enterprise to become competent as quickly as possible in all three disciplines: the foundation, risk governance process, and risk-aware culture. But that does not mean every enterprise needs to do it in the same way. Consider the following examples.

Royal Bank of Canada has created thorough, top-to-bottom governance arrangements for dealing with IT risk, including risks related to customer privacy as well as to IT operations. As described in the company's annual report, these highly structured arrangements place IT risk under the broader umbrella of enterprise risk management, which itself is structured into a hierarchy that includes nine major categories of risk.[1] Mechanisms for assessing and managing risk are comparable across every business unit, and decision-making committees are positioned at the business unit, group, and enterprise levels. It is a sophisticated, process-oriented approach to IT risk management, strongly supported by a comprehensive awareness program, and is considered by management to be an important part of the company's value proposition; among other things, company spokespersons have publicly attributed an estimated C$700 million in annual revenue to the company's privacy program.[2]

EquipCo is a global supplier of high-tech equipment and services.[3] Its governance arrangements are slender compared to Royal Bank of Canada's, but its awareness-based approach is strong. A global competency center staffed with thirty experts in various technical disciplines provides consulting expertise in IT risk management to business units throughout the company. Business units are encouraged to take responsibility for IT risk and to customize corporate policies to their own needs. Employees know that EquipCo's value proposition is about leading-edge design and safe, reliable products, and they take personal responsibility for securing EquipCo's intellectual property against threat and loss.

PartCo is a tier-two auto parts supplier.[4] It has grown at double-digit rates in the past five years by acquiring plants from automakers, refitting them to PartCo's specifications, and running them far more profitably than the previous owners. PartCo uses a single instance of its standard ERP software, running on a single brand and model of server, in every one of its factories. PartCo's infrastructure and applications base is so streamlined that the company can manage its worldwide IT capability with an internal organization of only forty people, supplemented by contractors as needed. PartCo's approach to IT risk management, in keeping with its overall corporate emphasis on lean manufacturing, is strongly oriented to the foundation discipline.

As these examples imply, every company that has excellent IT risk management tends to focus on one (or two) of the three risk disciplines, even as they bring all three up to speed. No enterprise has infinite attention or capabilities, and a focal point helps, especially at the start. The focal discipline builds attention and comfort with risk management throughout the enterprise, instilling it into the way the enterprise does business and helping make the case for changes that improve the other disciplines.

This is not to say that enterprises should focus on one discipline at the expense of others. All three disciplines are necessary to address the 4A's comprehensively—in terms of organization, technology, procedures, and behaviors. The enterprise must become *competent* in all three disciplines as fast as possible to ensure that dangerous gaps in IT risk management planning or execution have been eliminated. Then it should work diligently to continuously improve all three disciplines until they are truly excellent. The examples just cited, however, indicate that IT risk officers may choose to focus on one discipline to get a fast start and to sell the overall risk management program to the rest of the enterprise.

This begs at least two questions. What is the best focal discipline for my risk management program? What does it mean to be competent or excellent at each discipline?

The short answer to the first question is that enterprises should choose their focal discipline based on their culture, their circumstances, and their capabilities (not necessarily in that order). The goal is to make it as comfortable as possible for the enterprise as a whole to adopt risk management (and maybe even *want* to do risk management) so that it can become competent in all three disciplines as rapidly as possible. To answer the second question, let's consider what it means to be competent (or even excellent) in every discipline.

Achieving Competence with the Foundation

In the simplest terms, a competent foundation is one that is inherently resistant to common attacks and failures. This means, first, that the holes in the dike are plugged—that basic protections against attack and high-priority controls, as described in chapter 3, are in place. It also means that a business continuity plan is in place, is regularly tested, and is updated annually; that the enterprise has a technology architecture that is referenced in systems development and planning; and that the data center has a capable process for managing operations and assets. Finally, it means that there is a high-level plan for renewing and/or retiring complex and aging infrastructure and applications, and the enterprise is executing steadily against that plan. These behaviors and circumstances are evidence that the factors at the base of the risk pyramid are being actively managed.

The absence of any of these conditions means that significant risks can enter the base of the risk pyramid unobserved—in other words, that the foundation discipline is just not competent yet. To put it another way, you know your foundation discipline is not competent when you're constantly fighting fires; when unpleasant surprises, such as successful virus attacks and unplanned system downtime, are frequent; when you're constantly being told that your IT applications and infrastructures can't accommodate business plans in a timely, cost-effective way; and, in general, when IT is a hindrance rather than a help when big changes are under discussion.

Being competent is adequate for the short term—good enough to reduce firefighting and fix the major holes in the dike. But enterprises should keep improving, aiming to make the foundation as excellent as it can be. When the foundation discipline is excellent, in addition to the indications already cited, we would expect to see a ruthless implementation of architecture, which means that the enterprise has a simplified, standardized, highly functional infrastructure and application base and that deviations from the enterprise's chosen architecture are not allowed without an up-front analysis of the implications for future risk and cost. We would expect also to see a systematic, incremental renewal and a careful extension of the simplified foundation and ongoing investigation into advanced technologies with potential to either obsolete the firm's existing installed base or, alternatively, give the firm the potential to leapfrog its competition.

Achieving Competence with the Risk Governance Process

A competent risk governance process ensures that individual and group risk assessments are done regularly, so that the enterprise is not blindsided by risk and there are mechanisms in place to verify compliance to policy and handle exceptions. These goals are generally satisfied when a single person has been appointed to manage the risk governance process; formal risk categories have been identified and described in clear terms; a risk register is used to continuously record and track risks; consistent methods for risk assessment are in use and risk assessments are performed at least quarterly; tactical best practices for risk management, as described in chapter 5, are established; a multilevel risk governance arrangement—including councils for policy and implementation, executive sponsorship, and a team responsible for monitoring—is in place; and a formal process for resolving all or a majority of exceptions to IT risk policy has been established.

A clear leading indicator of a competent risk governance process is the percentage of executives at all levels who can accurately describe risk governance arrangements.[5] Executives who can't describe how risk governance works by definition don't have a clear idea of what risk governance demands of them and almost certainly don't know how well the process is working or what is being decided through it. In other words, if executives can't describe how the risk governance process works, it's probably not working.

You know that your risk governance process is not competent when no one knows who is in charge of it; neither risk categories nor assessment methods are standardized; there is no ongoing record of risk assessments and mitigation approaches; and no one can say for sure whether there is general compliance to policy.

When the governance process is the focal discipline, we would expect to see mandatory risk reviews of existing systems and systems under design and development; risk management incorporated into a wide range of business processes, such as due diligence reviews of new partnerships and service providers as well as mergers and acquisitions; integration of IT risk management into enterprise risk management councils; and ongoing measurement of the effectiveness of risk reduction efforts in terms of improved business performance. All of those indicators are representative of the practices that tend to satisfy auditor concerns about risk, which means that a competent IT risk governance process results in better audits—and that, in turn, produces less anxiety for everyone. Practices such as these are highly visible and demand considerable effort. For large financial services and pharmaceutical companies, and others for whom carefully calculated risk is a way of life, the effort is a relatively small price to pay to protect against bottomless risk.

Achieving Competence with the Risk-Aware Culture

Risk awareness is about culture—about values and beliefs and resulting behaviors. It's about more than knowing what risks are and how to handle them. A culture has competent risk awareness when it has a high degree of psychological safety where risk is concerned—when employees talk openly about risk and are comfortable asking for help in dealing with risks, including risks that pose difficult choices between uncertain outcomes.

When the enterprise is competent at risk awareness, risk discussions are an ongoing feature of senior executives' decision making. For example, discussions of new business initiatives include early assessments of potential IT risks and proposals for mitigating those risks effectively; project estimates are realistic and not padded to provide a huge margin for error at the expense of agility; critical success factors for projects are well known; and projects are subject to periodic review to ensure that critical success factors are maintained throughout them. Further, when risk awareness is competent, all IT and business executives can name the three top IT risks that apply within their scope of responsibility and can describe what steps are being taken to mitigate those risks, and all employees can name the IT risks that are most applicable to them and their business unit and can describe their own responsibilities related to those risks.

Risk awareness is not competent when employees hide risks instead of talking about them, even when asked; when project estimates are so heavily padded that it seems no work gets done; when the failure of infrastructure or projects leads first to finger-pointing and then to the resolution; when employees can't name the most important IT risks facing their business unit or describe what they can do to protect against those risks; when they don't know whom to call when they see something that might be a serious risk; and when management plans and strategies don't include explicit discussions of risks and contingency plans.

Similar to a competent risk governance process, competent risk awareness is just a starting point. When risk awareness is excellent, everyone in the organization is risk aware as a matter of course. Employees don't need to think about risk as a separate component of their explorations and decision making. It's just a natural part of everything they do. When risk awareness is excellent, we would expect to see frequent reminders of IT risk and controls via a variety of approaches, such as the periodic publication of risk metrics and discussions of progress about meeting key goals related to risk; periodic training for employees in risks and controls relevant to their roles and responsibilities; and streamlined mechanisms for reporting risk incidents to senior management with little "spin" or delay. We would expect senior executives to consider all aspects of IT risk—availability, access, accuracy, and agility—in their decisions and not simply trade off long-term problems for short-term convenience.

Finally, when risk awareness is excellent, we would expect executives to regularly look to the future, incorporating understandings of future scenarios and the associated risks into their strategic planning and strategic initiatives. We discuss looking forward at greater length in chapter 8.

Table 7-1 summarizes the characteristics of competence and excellence for all three disciplines.

TABLE 7-1

Competence and excellence for each IT risk management discipline

Discipline	Competent	Excellent
Foundation	• The holes in the dike are plugged. Basic protections against attack are in place. • A business continuity plan is in place, is regularly tested, and is updated annually. • The data center has a capable process for managing operations and assets, backed by solid monitoring. • The enterprise has enterprise and technology architectures that are referenced in all systems development and planning. • There is a high-level plan for renewing and/or retiring complex and aging infrastructure and applications, and the enterprise is executing steadily against the plan.	• Architecture has been ruthlessly implemented, with ongoing effort to simplify the foundation. • There is a systematic, incremental renewal and careful extension of this simplified foundation. • The enterprise continually investigates advanced technologies with the potential to obsolete the firm's existing installed base or give the firm the potential to leapfrog its competition.
Risk governance process	• A multilevel risk governance arrangement is in place. • A single person has been appointed to manage the risk governance process. • Formal risk categories have been identified and described in clear terms. • A risk register is used to record and track risks on an ongoing basis. • Consistent methods for risk assessment are in use, and risk assessments are being performed at least quarterly. • Tactical best practices for risk management are established. • A formal exception process is used to resolve all or a majority of exceptions to IT risk policy.	• Mandatory risk reviews of existing systems and systems under design and development. • The enterprise is continually measuring the effectiveness of risk reduction efforts. • IT risk management is incorporated into a wide range of business processes, such as due diligence reviews of new partnerships, service providers, and mergers or acquisitions. • IT risk management is fully integrated into enterprise risk management processes and councils.

Discipline	Competent	Excellent
Awareness	• Executives at all levels can describe the risk governance process accurately. • Employees talk openly about risk and are comfortable asking for help in dealing with risks. • Risk discussions are an ongoing feature of senior executives' decision making. Discussions of new business initiatives, for example, include early assessments of potential IT risks and proposals for mitigating those risks effectively. • Project estimates are realistic and not overly padded. Critical success factors for projects are well known, and every project is subject to periodic review to ensure that critical success factors are maintained throughout the project. • IT and business executives can name the top 3 IT risks that apply within their scope of responsibility and can describe what steps are being taken to mitigate those risks. • All employees can name the IT risks that are most applicable to them and their business unit and can describe their own responsibilities where those risks are concerned.	• There are frequent reminders of IT risk and controls via a variety of communications approaches, such as periodic publication of risk metrics and discussion of progress toward meeting key goals related to risk. • Employees are periodically trained in risks and controls relevant to their roles and responsibilities. • There are streamlined mechanisms for reporting risk incidents upward to senior management with a minimum of delay or "spin." • Employees at every level take direct responsibility for preventing, identifying, and dealing with risks. • Senior executives make a point of considering all aspects of IT risk in their decisions. • Executives look forward, incorporating understandings of future scenarios and the risks that go with them into long-range planning.

Culture, Circumstances, and Capabilities Affect the Focal Discipline

Culture, circumstances, and capabilities are the factors that matter most in choosing an enterprise's focal discipline. Which factor matters the *very* most in a particular case depends on the enterprise.

Because culture is notoriously difficult and time consuming to change—and not because it is necessarily the most important factor (it may not be for many enterprises)—we will discuss it first.

Organizational Culture Matters

We discussed the difficulty of changing culture in chapter 6. For the current discussion, it's enough to remember that a risk management discipline that runs counter to the organization's culture is a hard sell in any enterprise. And it's essential to be able to sell at least one discipline to the enterprise—so that it can be used to make all three effective. Culture can be changed, but not quickly or easily, and it is most successfully changed from the top down.

A culture that is conducive to a focus on its risk governance process is, above all, deliberate. It is comfortable with formal cooperation, committees, and task forces. It is accustomed to, and comfortable with, formal oversight and due process; it is used to documenting everything it does. It appreciates the value of a policy engine and is suspicious of "cowboys" who spurn it, whether openly or secretly. It is often routinely audited. Business units and individuals in such a culture are generally more willing to decide conflicts between corporate and business unit goals and principles in favor of the overall enterprise. Royal Bank of Canada, which, as we mentioned earlier, has made its privacy protections for customers a centerpiece of its value proposition, is an example of such a culture. Because regulators and auditors often require structure, documentation, and formal processes, enterprises in heavily regulated industries nearly always choose risk governance as their focal discipline.

A culture that is conducive to a focus on risk awareness is one in which expertise matters, consultants and internal experts are respected, and business unit independence and individual responsibility are important cultural values. The culture is sophisticated in terms of overall risks and their potential consequences and often has an explicit engineering-oriented culture. Such an enterprise is often more entrepreneurial than a culture that's oriented toward its risk governance process or foundation, and it tolerates a wider variety of products, missions, purposes, and approaches to doing business, rather than a tightly centralized, standardized process for doing business. EquipCo, which we mentioned at the start of this chapter, found that awareness best fit its culture.

A culture that is conducive to a focus on the foundation discipline is likely to be a start-up enterprise that has recently recreated itself (or is currently in the process of doing so), or one that made a decisive choice about its technology platform years ago and has taken care to stick to the path. Unity of culture, purpose, and direction are very strong. Agility matters, and very high efficiency is a close second. There may be only a few different types of product and service offerings, and the business model supports growth via the rapid replication of proven processes and technologies. ChipCo, already discussed in our chapter on the foundation discipline, is a clear example of the foundation as the focal discipline.

Some cultures are not particularly sympathetic to any of the disciplines; some cultures are basically tolerant of very high, even dangerous, levels of risk—in IT and elsewhere—and see controls as something to be evaded or ignored for reasons of necessity or advantage. There have been numerous examples in the press over the past few years. Serious risk management adoption in such enterprises usually occurs after a catastrophe and involves new management as well as a new culture. In these circumstances the risk governance process is the likely focus discipline, with awareness a close second; the process provides visibility, and awareness ensures that the process is followed scrupulously over the long term.

History Matters

An enterprise with a long history of poor foundation management, or an unnecessarily large and diverse base of applications and infrastructure, will find it profitable to improve matters via the foundation discipline—but making the foundation its focal discipline is often difficult. The necessary level of investment to rapidly transform the foundation is far too high for most boards of directors to accept. It is usually easier and less expensive to make process or awareness the focal discipline and use one of them to build momentum and make the case for investing in incremental foundation improvements.

EquipCo illustrates how history and culture can combine to push a company toward the awareness discipline. EquipCo's diverse business units operated on a global scale with an explicitly entrepreneurial approach to doing business, with each business unit encouraged to make its own successes in its own way, using its own preferred technologies. As a consequence, EquipCo's culture was generally wary of people from corporate, including those from the corporate IT group, and the overall foundation was very complex. For these reasons, the corporate IT group realized that a heavily centralized approach to either the risk governance or foundation disciplines was not an option.

However, EquipCo's employees had a great deal of security expertise because security was an important component of the value proposition for its products and services. And, as an engineering-focused company, people respected expertise and actively sought out help from well-known experts inside and outside the firm. The corporate IT group decided to leverage this culture and security expertise to improve awareness and then use awareness to gradually improve the effectiveness of the foundation and risk governance disciplines.

The corporate IT group built a very capable team of internal IT risk consultants—from inside and outside EquipCo—by recruiting experienced risk experts, each with a minimum of ten years' experience in a technical discipline and strong interpersonal skills. This thirty-person core risk group provided expertise and services in risk assessment and mitigation to the business unit IT groups. Members of this core group also worked as consultants to each business unit's IT director to prioritize risks and justify risk-related funding.

Instead of burdensome enterprise-level risk management processes, the team established competent corporate IT risk policies (e.g., standards for integrating supplier systems with internal systems) that business units could implement through customized local procedures. In addition, the corporate IT risk group actively assisted business units to help them grow their own risk expertise. The combination of a strong expertise-led awareness campaign and flexible risk governance process began to produce improvements to the risk profile of the foundation as well.

Over time, the activities of the core group increased awareness throughout the enterprise, and business units took responsibility for their own risk management work, reducing demand on the core group. This freed the core group to create more formal risk management processes. The group is now transitioning from conducting risk assessments to managing risk policy, process, and awareness programs. Its activities are improving the consistency of risk management and reporting throughout the enterprise, and providing advice and assistance as needed, while preserving the business units' independence.

Size Matters

Big companies tend to lead risk management with their risk governance process for several reasons. First, process is how big companies achieve economies of scale; process is something they understand well and seek to manage effectively. Second, huge installed bases of technology—which can vary widely in terms of make, model, and condition—often make it costly for big companies to make foundation simplification the focal discipline of their risk management efforts. As a result, such companies rapidly bring their foundation up to a competent level and then focus on one of the other disciplines to build momentum that helps improve the foundation incrementally to an excellent level. Process also improves awareness incrementally; as managers engage in risk governance processes, they come to understand conditions that create risk and activities that can reduce it, and they become comfortable identifying and sharing information about their risks.

Global companies tend to use their risk governance process to impose a minimal level of consistency on their risk management efforts worldwide, although we have seen risk awareness (often in the form of globally leveraged "competency centers" such as those that EquipCo used) fill this role as well. But with few exceptions, the bigger the company, the more likely that its risk governance process is the lead discipline.

Smaller companies tend to lead risk management with awareness or the foundation, depending on the age and complexity of their installed base (i.e., depending on the relative cost and difficulty of leading with their foundation). The relatively high inherent overhead for leading with process inhibits companies with fewer resources. If the company already has expert resources in place from successfully plugging the holes in its dike and if, like comparable companies, its smaller size means that its communications consume less overhead, making awareness the focal discipline can be the path of least resistance.

Industry Matters (But Not as Much as Size)

Any company that's regulated has to have some processes in place to comply with regulation. As of this writing, publicly traded companies worldwide, regardless of industry, are increasingly subject to financial reporting regulations similar to the U.S. Sarbanes-Oxley Act. But when an enterprise's core business processes and products, as opposed to its internal financial management, are regulated—as the financial services industry's are under Basel II, Gramm-Leach-Bliley, and the USA Patriot Act, and the U.S. health care industry's are under HIPAA—that's a strong indicator that the risk governance process is a good focal discipline. Regulation implies ongoing scrutiny, and scrutiny of this sort is largely satisfied by an observable process and the documentation that goes with it. The catch is that process always takes resources, and smaller businesses in even heavily regulated industries often hesitate to invest resources in nonrevenue-generating activities.

That said, enterprises in heavily regulated industries like financial services, pharmaceuticals, and health care—especially larger companies—tend to focus on their risk governance process almost by default. Large public sector enterprises, because of their usually mandatory requirements for thorough document and due process and their interest in emulating leading corporations, are increasingly focusing on their risk governance process as well.

Enterprises in mature industries—such as paper, steel, or insurance—tend to have substantial investments in a base of installed applications and infrastructures that defies simplification without further extensive investment. The sheer size of the sums involved tends to inhibit action unless a catastrophic event is imminent. (In some insurance companies, replacing core policy management applications is a billion-dollar investment—or more.) In such circumstances it's difficult to make foundation improvement the focal discipline once the foundation is at a competent level.

Some industries or enterprises are unpopular for social or political reasons. This includes public agencies devoted to taxation or defense, industries like tobacco whose license to operate may be in question, and enterprises whose success or methods inspire anger or jealously. In the Internet era such enterprises are subject to constant attack from a range of individuals and more organized groups. For example, Microsoft attracts upwards of eighty thousand external probes and attacks per day, a large number that is still less than the number of attacks on the U.S. Department of Defense.[6] Once the foundation is at a competent level, awareness is terrifically important—and a useful focal discipline—for an enterprise that is under constant attack from different directions.

Geography Matters

Particular countries and geography-based organizations impose their own regulatory requirements on enterprises and/or industries within their jurisdiction, including Gramm-Leach-Bliley, HIPAA, the Sarbanes-Oxley Act, and the USA Patriot Act in the United States; the Turnbull Report in the United Kingdom; the Data Protection Directive of the European Union; and literally dozens of others worldwide. Most requirements tend to involve extensive documentation, which is a hallmark of any risk governance process.

Geography also implies national or ethnic culture, and certain cultures tend more toward certain disciplines than others. For example, in Gartner surveys of IT project management practices, almost 100 percent of organizations responding in Australia had installed a project management office to manage methodology and support for project managers; for enterprises in the United States, Europe, Middle East, and Africa, the corresponding figure was closer to 50 percent.[7]

Capability Matters (Mostly at First)

Enterprise capabilities are powerful enablers and inhibitors—but they can change. Capabilities need not necessarily be built from the top of the enterprise down, and so they are easier to change than culture. For this reason, we believe that current capabilities should be considered mostly in terms of where the enterprise starts out, not where it intends to go—in other words, as a factor in planning the path to effective IT risk management and selecting a focus, not as the de facto end point.

Choose Your Focal Discipline

The checklists shown in tables 7-2a, b, and c can be used as a tool for thinking through the factors that would make one discipline or another a good focal point for your enterprise. We want to emphasize here that choosing a focal discipline does not mean that the other disciplines can be ignored. Without all three at competent levels, IT risk

TABLE 7-2A

Risk governance process checklist

Agree? (check)	Characteristic	Reasoning
☐	We customarily use committees and task forces to make policy decisions.	Indicates cultural fit with governance process
☐	We have formal processes for resolving policy exceptions.	Indicates cultural fit with governance process
☐	We use audits frequently to validate our processes.	Indicates cultural fit with governance process
☐	We actively enforce strong corporate standards and principles for behavior.	Indicates cultural fit with governance process
☐	Our core business processes and/or products and services (excluding financial management processes) are subject to regulation.	Often decisive factor for risk governance as lead discipline
☐	We have recently been subject to severe regulatory penalties, or our executives have been indicted or fired for ethical lapses.	Usually decisive factor for risk governance as lead discipline
☐	Our enterprise revenues (or budget, for a public agency) are greater than $1 billion.	Indicates that resources are sufficient to support risk governance process as lead discipline

management cannot be truly effective. We are saying only that, by focusing attention and effort on certain disciplines, enterprises can get the ball rolling with the focal discipline and use its momentum to make the case for improving the other disciplines as well.

Some factors strongly indicate that a particular discipline is in line with the enterprise's circumstances and should be the focus; others indicate that another discipline is *not* misaligned with the enterprise's circumstances and may be a good focus. The enterprise has not comprehensively addressed the organizational, technological, procedural, and behavioral aspects of IT risk management until it is at least competent in all three disciplines, and its focus may shift over time as circumstances and culture change.

In some cases enterprises will find that their needs, circumstances, and capabilities are at odds. To take an extreme example, if your CEO

TABLE 7-2B

Risk-aware culture checklist

Agree? (check)	Characteristic	Reasoning
☐	Proprietary expertise or intellectual property is critical to our success.	Strong potential for awareness as lead discipline
☐	We cultivate internal experts, such as engineers, and listen to them carefully.	Indicates cultural fit with awareness discipline
☐	We think about risk in everything we do and before we commit resources or make a decision to proceed.	Indicates cultural fit with awareness discipline
☐	We use a quality management approach such as TQM or Six Sigma to improve our operations and decisions.	Indicates cultural fit with awareness discipline
☐	We encourage business units to behave entrepreneurially and look out for themselves.	Emphasis on business units' independence is consistent with awareness as lead discipline, contrary to both governance process and foundation
☐	Our industry or company is a target for political or social activists or for criminals.	Focused targeting by activists or criminals requires heightened awareness
☐	We encourage employees at all levels to take personal responsibility for their actions and the results of those actions.	Indicates cultural fit with awareness discipline

Source: © 2007. MIT Sloan Center for Information Systems Research and Gartner, Inc. Used with permission.

or CFO has recently been indicted on charges related to misconduct or malfeasance, your enterprise is likely to be forced to focus on its risk governance process whether or not it's what you would choose. Given the will and the resources, capabilities can be acquired, as illustrated in earlier chapters when BOC acquired the ability to manage project risks and PFPC acquired the ability to manage its risk governance processes. Existing capabilities can be leveraged, improved, and augmented with external expertise and resources, if necessary.

TABLE 7-2C

Foundation checklist

Agree? (check)	Characteristic	Reasoning
☐	We have a focused and standardized technology base (e.g., one ERP instance worldwide).	Often decisive factor for foundation as lead discipline
☐	Our company built or rebuilt its technology base less than 10 years ago.	Strong potential for foundation as lead discipline
☐	Our technology base is supported by detailed, up-to-date documentation.	Strong potential for foundation as lead discipline
☐	We have an active portfolio management process and maintain an ongoing fund for renewing the installed base.	Strong potential for foundation as lead discipline
☐	We have a well-developed architecture that guides most or all of our systems acquisitions and development.	Potential for foundation as lead discipline
☐	Controlling costs through standardization of operations is a key company strategy	Indicates cultural fit with foundation discipline
☐	Our enterprise has plans or strategies that will require significantly retooling our technology base.	Retooling of technology base offers "green field" opportunity and strongly favors foundation discipline

Source: © 2007. MIT Sloan Center for Information Systems Research and Gartner, Inc. Used with permission.

Whatever the enterprise chooses as its focal discipline at the beginning of its journey to effective IT risk management, it must become competent in every discipline and continuously work to become excellent at all three. Enterprises should think of the focal discipline as a temporary focus that may shift as capabilities and needs change—which they will.

Comparisons of how two real-world companies chose their focal discipline should help illustrate the usefulness of the checklists in tables 7-2a, b, and c. We'll start with Shure, one of the world's leading manufacturers of professional and consumer sound reinforcement equipment. The company's microphones, such as the industry-standard SM57 and SM58, can be found in almost every professional recording studio in the world and on most concert stages. (An SM58 adorns the podium used by the president of the United States for press conferences.) The company is privately held. Hoovers.com reported sales of $245 million for Shure in 2006.

Shure: IT Risk and the Small Manufacturer

The importance of Shure's proprietary intellectual property is paramount.[8] "Managing intellectual property risk is part of the organizational DNA," says former CIO Paul Erbach. "We have a long history as a private company of being secretive, and we think of it as a competitive advantage." Shure's workforce has historically consisted of long-term, fanatically dedicated employees who design and build products on the job and use those products to make music on their own time. This is changing because Shure is setting up new manufacturing operations in China. According to Erbach, "Most employees have an average tenure of between 25 and 30 years. Now, as we open our plant in China, we're looking at people who've been with the company for just 25 to 30 days."

Limited resources are a challenge to implementing best practices. "We don't have a formal process for managing risk, or a formalized security officer role," says Erbach. "However, it's a well-defined part of the role of the director of technology. He's the chief infrastructure architect, manager of infrastructure services, and chief info security officer." Improving the company's approach to risks has meant pushing responsibility out to all employees. "When I got here, people were afraid to shut off services when there was a threat, so we established some empowerment parameters. We have very basic policies. We have disaster recovery procedures; we've implemented a three-year outside audit cycle; and we're working on a business continuity plan."

Shure is not a target for social or political activists, but the power of its brand attracts targeted attacks by profit-oriented criminals. "We've had problems with counterfeit Shure products," Erbach says. "That's a theft of intellectual property, but the means may be impossible to determine. It's the business changes, like building a new foreign plant, that drive us to rethink our protections."

Shure's profile on the risk discipline decision factors is shown in table 7-3. The table shows that Shure's decision to make awareness its focal discipline, with the foundation discipline a close second, is a good one. Shure is a manufacturer with an engineering orientation and a high corporate regard for the skills of the people who design and build its products. The company counts on the awareness of dedicated employees to protect its intellectual property. No long-time Shure employee would knowingly give away the design of the electronics inside a Shure microphone—or stand idly by while someone else did so.

With a recent ERP implementation completed and the need to control costs for the foreseeable future, Shure has an obvious second choice: the foundation discipline. The company's size, far under $1 billion in revenues, makes its governance process an unlikely candidate for the focal discipline. In a company this size—there are less than fifty IT employees—a competent process is lightweight indeed. This is especially true because, as a privately held company, Shure isn't required to adopt the process-related controls mandated for

TABLE 7-3

Focal IT risk discipline decision factors applied to Shure, Inc.

Agree?	Risk Governance Process
☐	We customarily use committees and task forces to make policy decisions.
☐	We have formal processes for resolving policy exceptions.
☐	We use audits frequently to validate our processes.
☐	We actively enforce strong corporate standards and principles for behavior.
☐	Our core business processes and/or products and services (excluding financial management processes) are subject to regulation.
☐	We have recently been subject to severe regulatory penalties, or our executives have been indicted or fired for ethical lapses.
☐	Our enterprise revenues (or budget, for a public agency) are greater than $1 billion.

	Awareness
☒	Proprietary expertise or intellectual property is critical to our success.
☒	We cultivate internal experts, such as engineers, and listen to them carefully.
☒	We think about risk in everything we do and before we commit resources or make a decision to proceed.
☒	We use a quality management approach such as TQM or Six Sigma to improve our operations and decisions.
☐	We encourage business units to behave entrepreneurially and look out for themselves.
☐	Our industry or company is a target for political or social activists or for criminals.
☒	We encourage employees at all levels to take personal responsibility for their actions and the results of those actions.

	Foundation
☐	We have a focused and standardized technology base (e.g., one ERP instance worldwide).
☒	Our company built or rebuilt its technology base less than 10 years ago.
☐	Our technology base is supported by detailed, up-to-date documentation.
☐	We have an active portfolio management process and maintain an ongoing fund for renewing the installed base.
☒	We have a well-developed architecture that guides most or all of our systems acquisitions and development.
☒	Controlling costs through standardization of operations is a key company strategy.
☐	Our enterprise has plans or strategies that will require significantly retooling our technology base.

Note: Authors' interpretation of the case study information.

publicly held U.S. companies under the Sarbanes-Oxley Act, and its core processes aren't regulated.

SAMPENSION: IT Risk and the Medium-Sized Pension Company

SAMPENSION is a Danish pensions company, created as a subsidiary of Kommunernes Pensionsforsikring A/S.[9] It is the common management company for three Danish pension funds, which together comprise about $15 billion in assets and a yearly revenue of $950 million. Hans-Henrik Mejloe has been CIO for six years. "We have the same pressures as many companies: to improve business processes, to adapt customer offerings and to respond to regulatory changes so we remain compliant and competitive," he says. "We had a lot of problems in the mid-1990s. Mainframe applications took years to develop, and government regulatory changes raised hurdles that looked almost impossible. We were forced to make radical changes."

The technology platform has since been transformed twice: from mainframe to client/server, and from client/server to a Windows platform. There are no applications more than eight years old. The main insurance application has been designed and rewritten to be flexible enough to support business strategy for the next five to ten years.

The IT organization bases its decisions on a set of thirteen maxims that commit the organization to a panorganizational architecture model, homogeneous technology, and strategic sourcing capabilities (including the capability to disengage from any vendor in two to three years). Every project goes through a formal process to ensure that it adheres to the maxims. IT staff are encouraged to develop cross-functional skills. Measurement processes pervade the IT organization: the IT unit measures and tracks items as diverse as application complexity; fixed costs; the unit's knowledge of the business and ability to deliver; and its competencies, motivation, and flexibility.

As shown in table 7-4, SAMPENSION's profile is oriented to both the risk governance process and the foundation. The first is

TABLE 7-4

Focal IT risk discipline decision factors applied to SAMPENSION

Agree?   Risk governance process

☒   We customarily use committees and task forces to make policy decisions.

☒   We have formal processes for resolving policy exceptions.

☒   We use audits frequently to validate our processes.

☒   We actively enforce strong corporate standards and principles for behavior.

☒   Our core business processes and/or products and services (excluding financial management processes) are subject to regulation.

☐   We have recently been subject to severe regulatory penalties, or our executives have been indicted or fired for ethical lapses.

☐   Our enterprise revenues (or budget, for a public agency) are greater than $1 billion.

Awareness

☐   Proprietary expertise or intellectual property is critical to our success.

☒   We cultivate internal experts, such as engineers, and listen to them carefully.

☐   We think about risk in everything we do and before we commit resources or make a decision to proceed.

☐   We use a quality management approach such as TQM or Six Sigma to improve our operations and decisions.

☐   We encourage business units to behave entrepreneurially and look out for themselves.

☒   Our industry or company is a target for political or social activists or for criminals.

☒   We encourage employees at all levels to take personal responsibility for their actions and the results of those actions.

Foundation

☒   We have a focused and standardized technology base (e.g., one ERP instance worldwide).

☒   Our company built or rebuilt its technology base less than 10 years ago.

☒   Our technology base is supported by detailed, up-to-date documentation.

☒   We have an active portfolio management process and maintain an on-going fund for renewing the installed base.

☒   We have a well-developed architecture that guides most or all of our systems acquisitions and development.

☒   Controlling costs through standardization of operations is a key company strategy.

☒   Our enterprise has plans or strategies that will require significantly retooling our technology base.

generally to be expected of a large financial services company; the second is not. Given the company's size and industry, the risk governance process is the likely lead discipline, with foundation a close second.

An enterprise should focus on its strengths, in risk management as in all things, and seek over time to minimize its vulnerabilities. That means focusing on a core risk management discipline that suits the enterprise's culture and strengths, ensuring that the other disciplines are at least competent and that it's improving all disciplines steadily over time.

No one of the risk disciplines is sufficient in itself, and competent execution of any risk discipline improves the effectiveness of all of them. An effective risk governance process increases awareness of risk at multiple levels, provides a forum for managers at various levels to discuss risk openly, and helps identify opportunities to piggyback on new initiatives to incrementally improve the foundation. Heightened risk awareness and the culture that goes with it make it more likely that managers will notice risks, bring them to the attention of governance councils, and cooperate to deal with them. It also makes managers more aware of the consequences of technology decisions that would introduce risk into the foundation. Efforts to improve the foundation, particularly through business continuity management and reviews of development projects, increase risk awareness and cooperation and help IT and business personnel understand the business consequences of IT risks in similar terms. In fact, several CIOs mentioned that, once the foundation and awareness were effective, the risk governance process could become less formal and burdensome while still maintaining its excellence.

Current capabilities matter most at the start as the organization learns or acquires the knowledge and skills it needs to execute well in areas that once were difficult. In the end, no enterprise should be satisfied with the minimum in any of its endeavors, including IT risk management.

This concludes our detailed discussion of how to build IT risk management capabilities that are right for the enterprise as it is today. In chapter 8, we describe how to ensure that your IT risk management capabilities continuously evolve to meet whatever challenges will face the enterprise in the future.

Eight

Looking Ahead

T O THIS POINT, we have concentrated on building an enterprisewide view of IT risk and risk management capabilities for businesses as they are today. But businesses and the environments in which they operate change, and those changes introduce new risks and alter the priorities of older ones. Business and technology change too quickly to rely on reactive approaches to managing IT risk—reactive management is ineffective management and results in the loss of too many opportunities and the realization of too many threats.

The most dangerous risks are the ones that are never considered or that are considered too late. If a reactive approach is too slow for the pace of business, businesses must look ahead to anticipate the IT risks of the future.

Look to the Future in the Right Order

IT risk is business risk with business consequences, and changes in the business and its environment will affect an enterprise's overall risk profile. Risk managers need a way to examine changes on the horizon and take appropriate action. Accordingly, looking to the future begins by examining the IT risk trade-offs implied by the company's business strategy and its environment and framed in terms of the 4A's. The outcome is a set of strategies for controlling risks. These, in turn, are used to drive necessary changes to the three disciplines, as shown in figure 8-1.

FIGURE 8-1

Planning sequence for strategic IT risk management

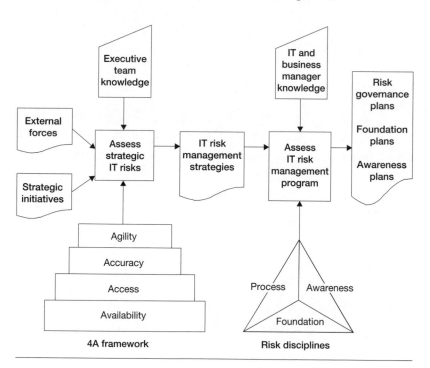

Look to External Forces and Strategic Initiatives

This is not a book on strategic planning, and we offer no advice here on the methods executives might use to scan the competitive environment or develop future visions, strategies, and plans. For this discussion, we will assume that the business has a strategy and that its IT capabilities have already been incorporated into that strategy (at least in the sense that the strategy explicitly recognizes the most essential technology capabilities required, if not exactly how they will be acquired). It goes without saying that IT executives should be participants in those discussions.

The questions used by executives to identify and assess potential IT risks to the strategy are the same as those described in chapter 1 for setting high-level risk priorities, but the focus is on the enterprise and its environment *as they will be*, not as they are. These conversations are more or less extensive and frequent, depending on the extent of change contained in the strategy and the business's environment. For most enterprises right now, the pace of change means that annual conversations about these issues are not frequent enough.

Look for Signs of New or Changing External Forces

Discussions of future risks and their implications begin with the most important external forces that might affect a broad range of enterprise initiatives. These forces may be threats, but they may also be opportunities. Members of the executive team can start with the forces that are most apparent to them. In addition, they can call on internal and external resources to identify external forces that will have an important impact but that do not yet appear to be directly relevant to the casual observer. Many external forces apply to an enterprise, and an enterprise will be affected by (or benefit from) each one differently.

As a generalized example that affects almost every enterprise, we focus on the potential for regulatory change, keeping in mind that it is just one of many potential external forces that influence IT risk. Although some firms treat regulatory risk as a separate category in their enterprise risk framework, we believe that regulatory risk, in IT terms, is really about the 4A's. Some examples include:

- The Sarbanes-Oxley Act requires businesses to control accuracy risks, which affects the control of access and availability risks as well.

- HIPAA, U.S. state laws based on California's State Bill 1386, and regulations such as the European Union's Data Protection Directive force enterprises to control privacy, a particular form of access risk, on behalf of their customers.

- Large financial services businesses are further subject to regulations that enforce protections against loss of availability—for example, requirements for off-site storage of data backups—and to accuracy-oriented regulations such as Basel II and the USA Patriot Act.

Regulation is usually a reactive response to a perceived threat to society and so is often preceded by visible warning signs of the change to come. As an example, the passage of California's State Bill 1386 and its enforcement (beginning in July 2004), and the nearly immediate wave of high-profile publicity for data thefts in a wide range of consumer-facing businesses that followed, was a warning signal that access risks (and, in particular, the risk of identity theft) had increased significantly for individuals and, as a result, for businesses that handle personal information. By heeding that signal and adjusting business processes and IT risk governance accordingly, data brokers might have avoided scrutiny from U.S. legislators in the wake of ChoicePoint's inadvertent and highly publicized sale of personal and financial information for more than a hundred fifty thousand individuals to criminals in February 2005.[1] Potential restrictions on industry agility, as of this writing, include two bills before the U.S. Congress that would for the first time impose specific requirements for data management and information security on the data broker industry.[2]

Similarly, the continuing high frequency and increasing impact of technology-related failures, a few examples of which were described in the introduction, might be an early warning sign to the IT industry that the potential for regulation of IT vendors, their products, and their services (in addition to their enterprise customers) is growing. In this case, at least one business is already taking action. Microsoft's enormous (over $100 million in the first six months) and very public investment in its Trustworthy Computing initiative—which aims to improve security, reliability, and privacy (access and availability) protections in its operating systems and applications—can be interpreted as a strategic response designed to reduce the potential for formal regulation (and the resulting loss of agility) of the industry in which Microsoft is a leading player. It can also be viewed as an effort to reverse the increasing loss of goodwill from the enterprises and individuals who use Microsoft products—that is, the vast majority of personal computer users worldwide.

Like Microsoft's Trustworthy Computing initiative, strategic responses to external forces for regulation may be very demanding. Without a well-structured foundation, each new regulation can become a burdensome drain on the enterprise.

Especially when the foundation has been neglected for years in favor of reduced costs, the business and IT costs to address availability, access, and accuracy risks may be large enough to change corporate strategy or reprioritize major initiatives (as they were for Tektronix and other examples in this book). More than a few companies have speeded up their plans to replace aging applications in response to Sarbanes-Oxley; at least one company known to us chose instead to take a calculated risk, adhering to a schedule for ERP implementation that lagged Sarbanes-Oxley compliance dates by years rather than pay twice to comply (once for a stopgap solution, and a second time for ERP). Executives in some publicly traded companies chose to take their companies private rather than undertake the effort and expense necessary to comply with Sarbanes-Oxley.[3] Some banks have reported costs of up to 15 percent of their IT budget—hundreds of millions of dollars in some cases—for complying with Basel II requirements (and those are only the IT costs).[4] This is all the more reason for companies to pay attention to early warning signs that external forces may be increasing IT risks—and, of course, to consider investing in a foundation that responds more easily to change when change is necessary, as opposed to stopgap solutions that complicate the foundation and must be redone for every new regulatory mandate.

Look at Strategic Initiatives

Although external forces are important influences on IT risk, internal forces are just as important. Major strategic initiatives—such as new partnerships (e.g., for outsourcing, developing products, and marketing joint ventures), new product or service offerings, and expansions to new markets or customers—carry important IT risk implications. We explore some of these examples in greater depth here.

Partnerships of all kinds have significant implications for IT risk. Outsourcing IT and business services, such as data center or call center management or application development, reduces availability risk and agility risk by transferring risk to partners who can manage them more cost-effectively. Joint ventures aim to reduce agility risk by leveraging the complementary strengths of the parties involved. Both potentially open the doors of the enterprise to new availability, access, and accuracy risks, and executives must consider how such risks can be mitigated. For example, will external partners be required to meet or exceed internal standards for availability, access, and accuracy controls? (The usual answer is yes.) If supply chain partners are given access to the company's systems, how will it ensure that the information provided doesn't wind up in the hands of competitors? How can a partner's compliance with the company's standards be ensured and measured? Executives don't need to consider detailed answers to those questions, but they need to know whether answers exist and to support the changes to risk governance, the foundation, and awareness necessary to implement and enforce those answers.

When audio equipment manufacturer Shure opened manufacturing operations in China, it reduced costs and expanded its manufacturing base. At the same time, the company increased access risks by exporting valuable intellectual property—industry-leading microphone designs—to a region notorious for its disregard for intellectual property rights.[5] Controlling those risks meant installing new information technology controls at the company's factories in China, such as security add-ons to computer-aided-design systems to restrict access to designs (or parts of designs) based on the user's job role. It also meant training Shure personnel to classify the security levels of microphone designs piece by piece so that access could be restricted, something very new for a company that had traditionally relied on the loyalty of its mostly long-time employees to protect its intellectual property.

New or radically changed product and service offerings, especially those involving new channels or incorporating information and communications technologies, raise similar questions. To what extent do the new products and services create availability, access, or accuracy risk for the business or its customers—because of the characteristics of the product itself, the information contained in the product, or the systems that support the product? For example, when a financial services company enables customers access to their accounts electronically, how can the firm ensure security both for itself and its customers (in other words, how can it reduce access risks to an acceptable level)? Will customers expect the firm to do so? Will competitors encourage such expectations? What will happen if the firm fails to meet those expectations? For example, some firms, such as Bank of America and Yahoo!, have taken steps to improve online access risk beyond typical user IDs and passwords.[6] They now allow their customers to choose a customized image—known only to the firm and the customer—that appears on the firms' Web pages. If customers don't see the icon, they know that something is wrong and can end their Web site visit before handing personal or account information over to a spoofed site.

Then consider availability risk: Can the firm ensure that accounts are available around the clock for viewing online? Is that kind of guaranteed availability something new for the enterprise? Will the current foundation support it?

In a product initiative, if the firm sells intelligent devices that customers will use to store important personal information, can it protect the information in the device even if the device is lost or stolen? If devices contain technology to allow users to communicate wirelessly, can the firm protect the device and its owner from unwanted or hostile communications? Will customers expect either of those protections? Will competitors be able to promise them?

Asking and answering questions such as these in a new or up-dated product or service launch can prevent future consequences for both customers and the company. In late 2005, an independent computer security expert announced to the world that Sony Music, to protect its music CDs against unauthorized duplication, had embedded a "rootkit" on them—computer code that secretly replaced key operating system components on personal computers that played the disks.[7] The purpose of the rootkit was to allow Sony to surreptitiously monitor the modified computers for illegal copying of Sony CDs. Unfortunately for all concerned, the rootkits gave criminal hackers the means to easily seize control of infected computers for their own criminal purposes, and many customers found it extremely difficult to remove the modified operating systems components from their machines. Once revealed, the incident exposed Sony to hostile attention worldwide from security experts, the press, Sony customers and other music fans, and government agencies (including the U.S. Department of Homeland Security, which apparently considered the incident a possible matter of national security). Multiple lawsuits against Sony—some of which have, as of this writing, yet to be settled—tarnished the firm's reputation and the music industry's efforts to counter piracy of its products. It seems likely that the company had not thought through the potential IT risks for itself, its customers, and its industry in a strategic initiative designed to thwart a growing wave of intellectual property theft.

New markets or customers may involve the business in different regulatory regimes that reflect different risk tolerances. Does speed matter more than customer service? Does cost or access to markets matter more than privacy (a trade-off that was considered in the Virtual Services, Inc. case described in chapter 1)? One insurance company's initiative to sell a new line of variable life insurance products brought it into conflict with the Securities and Exchange Commission when its aging policy administration systems were unable to produce timely, accurate reports on the investment components of its policies. In this case the only acceptable solution was to pay for upgrades to the systems. The impact of this trade-off between accuracy risks and agility risks on the business case would have been more palatable to management if it had been examined earlier.

In April 2001, Amazon.com announced retroactive changes to its privacy policy that allowed it to share customer data, including data about customer purchases, with selected business partners. Customers could choose not to do business with Amazon going forward, but that would not prevent the company from using the data already gathered in any way it deemed appropriate. This act was a calculated risk that apparently paid off.[8] When Google expanded its operations to China, the company found that Chinese authorities had a dim view of unrestricted search capabilities where Chinese citizens were concerned. Google's decision—to accede to the Chinese government's requirements by imposing unique search restrictions on users based in China—balanced the agility risks of potentially being excluded from the world's fastest-growing market against the uproar that might (and did) result in its home markets from violating Western democratic societal norms for access, privacy, and freedom of speech (and, possibly, the company's own cherished maxim: "Don't be evil").[9]

Examining the availability, access, accuracy, and agility risk implications of new strategic business initiatives arms the executive team to deal with the associated IT risks. The executive team can explicitly recognize the trade-offs and contingencies that are necessary to success and those adjustments that must be made to current risk tolerances on the 4A's. The next step? The rest of the enterprise must translate those strategies into a set of initiatives in the IT risk management program, including changes to the three disciplines of risk management: the foundation, risk governance process, and risk awareness.

Look to the Three Disciplines

Operationalizing a strategy for IT risk management means incorporating it into the enterprise's foundation, risk governance process, and risk awareness programs—the three disciplines:

- Where the foundation is concerned, compare the new IT risk strategy to the current base of infrastructure and applications and the people and processes that support them. If gaps exist between desired capabilities and current capabilities, managers must either address the gaps or change the strategy for risk management (and potentially the strategic initiative itself). For example, if the risks cannot be absorbed by the foundation, the enterprise may need to adjust its tolerance for risks to the 4A's or modify the initiative's value proposition for customers, distributors, or the company.

- Where the risk governance process is concerned, governance bodies at all levels must be informed of the new priorities. Policy-making bodies may need to change or create policy or to charter and approve funding for new projects; implementation councils may need to define and implement new standards or modify existing ones and to track the progress of such efforts; monitoring bodies may need to ensure that criteria for assessing systems are updated to reflect revised policies and standards. Risk assessment procedures may need to change, and managers using those procedures may need instruction in how to implement such changes.

- Where risk awareness and risk-aware culture are concerned, affected employees must be informed of new risk priorities and the rationale behind them, and managers at all levels must show support in word and deed.

The case of OSF HealthCare shows many of these effects on the three disciplines in action.[10] OSF is a $2.5 billion corporation operating an integrated network of health care facilities in Illinois and Michigan. Michael Nauman has been the company's CIO for about four years; before taking on that role, Nauman was the administrator of operations at the largest OSF hospital. "In 2000, the majority of the IT asset base at OSF was dedicated to the revenue cycle," Nauman told us in early 2006. "Operationally, the IT base required significant investment to keep up with various near-future regulatory issues." Other external forces beyond regulation were driving OSF and the industry to change as well, increasing pressure on the health care industry to improve quality of care and to lower costs, in large part by shifting its traditional focus on IT for administrative systems to IT for clinical support in such areas as diagnosis.

It took time to build consensus for major changes to the foundation among the OSF leadership team, even though there was general agreement that change was needed. "The technology we were riding on was seen as a barrier for clinical transformation," Nauman said. "The IT performance gap was the focus of most discussions. It was the key barrier in the minds of senior leadership. And in a strategic sense, that was a fair perception. At our spending level, the quality of our environment should have been on par with the best in the industry, but instead we were among the worst. IT was perceived as being out of sync, and we needed to refocus efforts on funding industry solutions that addressed our clinical needs and our desire to be a leader in future technology to support our caregivers." The alternative was increased risk to agility resulting from failure to address the efficiency and effectiveness issues driving the industry.

In 2001, a team composed of senior hospital leaders, including Nauman, assessed the application portfolio and began planning an $80 million project to replace legacy infrastructure and applications. As the project matured and was approved by the board, the group functioned as an organizing committee, ensuring ongoing executive support and further reducing project risk.

Significant changes were made to simplify the foundation. "We went from a 'best-of-breed' to a 'best-of-cluster' strategy," Nauman said. "At OSF it's all about practicality and stewardship for our IT investments. We need stability, reliability and performance. When it came to the core Hospital Information System, we needed something that would scale from a 50-bed hospital to a 750-bed hospital. We went from six nonintegrated database management systems to one. We replaced the care delivery side, the resource management side and the revenue cycle side—those basic large buckets. All the revenue cycle systems were replaced with PeopleSoft. We replaced billing and admitting systems and integrated those with the clinical and ancillary systems."

Management used governance and awareness programs to change culture and keep the newly simplified foundation clean and IT risks low. According to Nauman, "We went from an IT culture where diversity in systems was celebrated, to one in which you needed to show that our chosen standard technology would not do the job before you were able to choose a nonstandard option."

With the new foundation in place, management is looking further into the future. "My operating budget right now is 3.8 percent of the total organization's operating budget," Nauman said. "In 2001, it was 3.9 percent. We're paying about the same, but the number of user devices supported has increased by 150 percent and the quality is much better. We are able to offer better solutions for our business and clinical needs, but we now must move into being able to help our business units anticipate new technology needs, and assist them in planning for a future where technology will play a major role in supporting our caregivers' decision-making needs. We need to do a little more frontier work so we can continue to provide creative solutions and stay in step with technology innovations."

Just as no enterprise or its environment is ever static, no risk management strategy can be fixed forever. Most enterprises engage in ongoing strategic change, and their IT risk management strategies must be examined regularly for the implications of those changes.

Looking forward essentially means asking questions to explore the ways in which the company plans to engage with its customers, competitors, partners, and environment; understanding the changes to existing IT risks implied by those exchanges; and making sure that the enterprise follows up to reduce exposure to risky situations. In the end, it's simply one more way to ensure that the enterprise has taken care to avoid the consequences of dangerous surprises.

This completes our detailed discussion of the two frameworks—the 4A's and three core disciplines—that are the basis of capable IT risk management. In the final chapter, we briefly summarize these concepts in a set of ten ways that executives can improve IT risk management.

Nine

Ten Ways Executives Can Improve IT Risk Management

S OME BIRTHDAY PARTIES are surprises. All ambushes are. Where IT risk is concerned, a surprise is usually more like an ambush than a party. If your IT risk management is working, you are rarely ambushed by unpleasant surprises with your enterprise's technology. If you are experiencing frequent unpleasant surprises, or you have reached the point where IT's underperformance and failure are no longer surprising to you, then your IT risk management isn't working, and you need to fix it before you get a dangerously big surprise.

In this book we have described two important and complementary approaches to managing IT risk for competitive advantage. The 4A's (availability, access, accuracy, and agility) represent the most pressing enterprise-level objectives affected by IT risk. Classifying and assessing risks in terms of the 4A's sets the organization up for success. Business executives can comfortably manage IT risks in the same way they manage all risks: by making informed choices between business alternatives.

But this is just a start. Discussing risk is not managing risk. Risks are managed by the whole organization, using the capabilities embodied in the three core disciplines of the foundation, risk governance process, and awareness. The foundation discipline reduces basic IT risks and more. It embodies the risk trade-offs and tolerances that flow from executive-level discussions of the 4A's: prioritizing some processes over others, making information more global or more compartmentalized, promoting standardization or local flexibility. The risk governance process allows managers at all levels to identify and assess risks on the 4A's and to ensure that they are managed appropriately. Awareness builds on the risk tolerances established in executive-level conversations and then goes a step further to help all employees recognize risky conditions, avoid risky behaviors, and jointly take responsibility for risk-smart actions.

The 4A's and three core disciplines establish effective risk management for today that will continue to be effective for tomorrow. In chapter 8, we described how some important trends of tomorrow may impact IT risk and how to consider them in terms of the 4A's and core disciplines. We will close this book with a brief reminder of ten ways executives can improve IT risk management.

1. Treat IT risk as business risk

Every IT risk has a business consequence. Small incidents often signal larger problems, and a series of small IT decisions can lead to large levels of risk to the business. A potential technology failure that can have serious consequences for the business is never minor, no matter how ordinary or normal it may seem. Managing risk—including IT risk—is a key fiduciary responsibility of every executive. Risk should be part of every conversation about overseeing IT.

2. Consider risks in terms of the 4A's—for both the long term and the short term

Short-term decisions made locally have long-term consequences for the overall enterprise. The consequences of decisions about IT risk play out in the 4A's over time. No executive can understand the real meaning of an IT risk until she has examined its longer-term consequences in the 4A's for the entire enterprise.

Most technical decisions involve conscious or unconscious trade-offs among the 4A's. If executives don't make the trade-offs and risk tolerances clear, lower-level employees will make decisions based on whatever assumptions they have gleaned from previous decisions. It's much better to consciously understand and debate the trade-offs than it is to be surprised later by the results of someone else's decision. This is especially important for fast-growing enterprises or enterprises undergoing major change, where the "standard operating procedure" may no longer be the appropriate.

3. Plug the holes in the dike, and be ready for more floods

The first step in reducing IT risk is to make sure the existing foundation is as strong as it can be. Persistent leaks or cracks in a foundation can bring down even the strongest structure. Start with business continuity management, an engine that pulls a very long train. It identifies issues in the foundation and improves the risk governance process and risk awareness throughout the enterprise while reducing the potential impacts of unavoidable incidents. At the same time, identify and plug any visible holes in the foundation that have resulted from sloppiness, inattention, poor structure, or lack of internal controls. Using IT audit to thoroughly identify gaps and controls and implementing industry best practices are good ways to start the process.

4. Simplify the foundation

A simplified foundation works better, costs significantly less to own and operate, is more flexible, fails less often, and is fixed more easily when it fails. Consolidate and simplify the infrastructure until it's as standardized and lean as it can get. Few enterprises can afford not to simplify infrastructure based solely on the financial merits.

Infrastructure simplification can happen quickly under the CIO's control with relatively little disruption to business processes. Simplifying applications is more difficult because applications are intimately tied to business processes. When the risk of living with the firm's existing applications outweighs the risk of replacing them, a rapid transformation—quickly replacing all applications, with all the risk and organizational trauma that implies—may be in order. But in most cases, the case for application simplification is less immediately pressing, and enterprises replace them gradually, one project at a time.

5. Create risk governance structures and process; embed IT risk management into every other business process and decision

The core dilemma of IT risk management is that the people most able to make enterprise-level decisions about risk trade-offs are those least capable of understanding or addressing detailed risks throughout the enterprise. Managers deep in the enterprise have the detailed knowledge necessary to identify and address risks, but lack the enterprise-level perspective that higher-level executives have (and vice versa). Without a risk governance process, the blind men will never understand the elephant, and people with differing risk tolerances will never come to agreement. By embedding IT risk management into key decision processes, the enterprise avoids being blindsided and can take on more risk, and therefore more opportunity, with greater confidence. A risk governance process provides a picture of all risks facing each level of the enterprise so that decision makers can compare them, decide what to do about them, and see that they have been managed. A risk governance process also creates a sense of order and control—it instills confidence, inside and outside the enterprise, that risk is being managed appropriately. For these reasons, a risk governance process—with all the effort, investment, people, and policy required—is more than a bureaucratic effort. It keeps everything moving smoothly so that risk management becomes just another part of doing business.

6. Give every employee appropriate awareness of the risks, vulnerabilities, and policies that matter most to them

An enterprise whose employees do not know or understand IT risk is a vulnerable enterprise. The power of modern technology is immense and highly distributed by its nature, no matter what the enterprise's mission or culture happens to be. Employees at every level must know how to use IT safely, what danger looks like for them and their responsibilities, how policies and standards reduce vulnerabilities, and what to do when danger (such as an out-of-control foundation or a contractor behaving irresponsibly) appears. Process goes a long way to improving awareness by making risk-aware actions part of daily life. But training and frequent communication is also essential. Our research shows that awareness training is associated with statistically significantly lower risk to each of the 4A's. People in different parts of the enterprise need to be aware of different elements of IT risk, but all need to be aware.

7. Create a risk-aware culture

A culture that doesn't feel safe talking about risk can't stop risk; it can only suffer the consequences. Risk-averse people often avoid sharing information about risks, leading to costly incidents when risks exceed the control of a single individual. Or they resist taking useful business risks, increasing risk to agility.

A risk-aware culture starts at the top. Only executives can create a culture in which everyone in the enterprise feels free to talk openly about risk, to take calculated risks, and to work together to bring unacceptable risks down to acceptable levels. Executives do this by asking about risk regularly, publicly rewarding risk-conscious actions, and demonstrating through their own behaviors that risk awareness should be part of the culture.

8. Measure effectiveness

You can't prove that something never happened because of your IT risk program, but you can measure the effort you put into your program, the frequency and business impact of incidents, key risk indicators, general and role-specific levels of awareness, and the agility that the enterprise gains by improving its IT risk profile. Service levels and business efficiencies are not the issue; vulnerability and risk are. Use measures to drive awareness, process, and foundation simplification; and demonstrate to people inside and outside the enterprise that risk management capability and business performance enabled by a stronger foundation are improving every day.

9. Look forward

A well-designed risk management capability makes the firm more agile to venture into the future. But many changes in the future will impact the firm's risk profile or require adjustment to its risk tolerance and trade-offs. When considering future trends or implementing a major new initiative, be sure to discuss how the 4A's will be impacted and how the three disciplines should change to anticipate that change. Don't predict the future; imagine the future and the risks that it poses, and define the strategies and actions that will help you thrive then.

10. Lead by example

Executives set the tone for the cultures they lead. Leaders must make it clear to everyone in the enterprise by deed as well as by word that risks are to be faced *openly*. All employees, regardless of job description, can set an example for their colleagues by sounding the alarm when risk appears, by acknowledging their concerns about their own risks, and by asking for help when they need it. Living the behaviors that exemplify risk management is a good way to convince doubters that risk management need not be an onerous extra burden but rather just another part of doing business.

Until the enterprise has IT risk under control, the value represented by the business processes that IT supports and enables is inherently at risk. In a world where almost every business process and relationship is supported by IT, there is much more at stake in managing IT risk than the dollars the enterprise has invested in technology.

Executives talk about risk every day. Every successful executive takes risks and manages them effectively to earn above-normal returns. But few people enjoy talking about risk. The discussions are demanding and uncomfortable. They are about making choices between less-than-optimal outcomes, with less information than participants would like.

We can't promise that this book will help you enjoy talking about IT risk, but we do hope that the tools and examples we've provided will make you more comfortable having those conversations.

After all, it is those conversations that turn risk management from a dreadful necessity to a source of competitive value. Executives who think of IT risk only in terms of pure risk aversion—terms that are appropriate to dealing with hazardous chemicals or preparing consolidated financial reports—leave value on the table that less risk-averse competitors can choose to exploit.

When IT risk is handled as a compliance issue, it's just a cost to be managed. But if IT risk is handled in the right way—by building the three risk management disciplines and discussing IT risk in business terms using the 4A's—it becomes more than that. It returns business value in three ways: by reducing IT "fires," by making the IT foundation more efficient, and by enabling the enterprise to pursue valuable business opportunities that competitors would consider too risky to attempt.

In other words, an enterprise that manages IT risk effectively is not just a safer enterprise—it is a more agile enterprise. With that, we wish you success in turning IT risk into competitive advantage.

Notes

Introduction

1. Stephanie Overby, "Bound to Fail," *CIO*, May 1, 2005; and Bob Driehaus, "How It Happened: Onslaught Overtaxed an Old Computer," *Cincinnati Post*, December 28, 2004.

2. Ibid.

3. Ibid

4. Ibid.

5. Information on Tektronix throughout this book is derived from a case study written by George Westerman, Mark Cotteleer, Robert Austin, and Richard Nolan. "Tektronix, Inc.: Global ERP Implementation," Case 9-699-043 (Boston: Harvard Business School, 1999) as well as the case teaching note, Robert D. Austin, "Tektronix, Inc.: Global ERP Implementation," Teaching Note 5-602-078 (Boston: Harvard Business School, 2001), and Tektronix Annual Reports from 1999–2001.

6. Robert McMillan, "Troubled CardSystems to Be Sold," *InfoWorld*, September 23, 2005; "CardSystems Sold to California Company," *Atlanta Business Chronicle*, September 23, 2005.

7. Dale Buss, "Nightmare," *Context Magazine*, Spring 1998.

8. David Hencke, "Revenue Lost Up to £2bn in Tax Credit Shambles," *Guardian*, November 20, 2003.

9. Widespread public disclosure of IT risk events is a relatively new phenomenon, a result of instantaneous global communications and increased corporate and personal transparency—what Richard referred to as a "world without secrets" in his book of the same name: Richard Hunter, *World Without Secrets* (New York: Wiley, 2002).

10. Our survey analysis shows that these factors are statistically significantly correlated to increased IT risk. We will discuss details in chapters 3–6.

11. Eddie George, *Report of the Banking Supervision Inquiry into the Circumstances of the Collapse of Barings, Ordered by the House of Commons* (London: Her Majesty's Stationery Office, July 1995).

12. Westerman et al., "Tektronix, Inc."; Austin, "Tektronix, Inc." Teaching Note; and Tektronix Annual Reports from 1999–2001.

Chapter 1

1. There are many effective CIOs and other senior IT managers who are able to put technical considerations into business language and show how IT decisions relate to business difficulties or benefits. But lower-level IT people often have problems with this. And even the most business-focused IT managers can have difficulty discussing IT risk in purely business terms. That's one purpose of this book: to help business and IT people find a common language to discuss IT risks and the subsequent business consequences.

Looking back, we could debate how important on-the-spot support was at 2 a.m. in the Internet world of 1997, but, ultimately, that is not for us, as outsiders, to judge. Discussing the likelihood and impact of the 4A's in business terms can help business and IT people work together and make appropriate trade-offs that go beyond looking only at costs. Making the optimal decision is less important than making a decision that balances risks to the satisfaction of all.

2. The 4A framework builds on the framework originally developed in George Westerman, "Understanding the Enterprise's IT Risk Profile," Research Briefing IV(1C) (Cambridge, MA: Center for Information Systems Research, MIT Sloan School of Management, March 2004). It was subsequently refined in publications such as Richard Hunter, George Westerman, and Dave Aron, "IT Risk Management: A Little Bit More Is a Whole Lot Better," Research Report (Stamford, CT: Gartner Executive Programs, February 2005); and George Westerman, "IT Risk Management: From IT Necessity to Strategic Business Value," working paper 366, Center for Information Systems Research, MIT Sloan School of Management, Cambridge, MA, December 2006.

3. Some companies may choose to add another enterprise objective to this list, but the 4A's represent a concise, clear set of the most important enterprise objectives affected by IT. If you add another objective, be careful that it's really independent. For example, reputation risk is actually a risk derived from one or more of the 4A's, depending on which is more important for the enterprise and its customers. Making reputation a separate risk may make risk management trade-offs more complicated with little extra benefit to the enterprise.

4. George Westerman, Mark Cotteleer, Robert Austin, and Richard Nolan, "Tektronix, Inc.: Global ERP Implementation," Case 9-699-043 (Boston: Harvard Business School, 1999); Robert D. Austin, "Tektronix, Inc.: Global ERP Implementation," Teaching Note 5-602-078 (Boston: Harvard Business School, 2001); and Tektronix Annual Reports from 1999–2001.

5. Hunter, Westerman, and Aron, "IT Risk Management: A Little Bit More Is a Whole Lot Better."

6. Richard Woodham and Peter Weill, "Manheim Interactive: Selling Cars Online," working paper 314, Center for Information Systems Research, MIT Sloan School of Management, Cambridge, MA, February 2001.

7. Ibid.

8. Virtual Services, Inc. is a pseudonym.

Chapter 2

1. The three core disciplines draw on a framework originally developed in George Westerman, "Building IT Risk Management Effectiveness," Research Briefing IV(2C) (Cambridge, MA: Center for Information Systems Research, MIT Sloan School of Management, July 2004). It was subsequently refined in publications such as Richard Hunter, George Westerman, and Dave Aron, "IT Risk Management: A Little Bit More Is a Whole Lot Better," Research Report (Stamford, CT: Gartner Executive Programs, February 2005); and George Westerman, "IT Risk Management: From IT Necessity to Strategic Business Value," working paper 366, Center for Information Systems Research, MIT Sloan School of Management, Cambridge, MA, December 2006.

2. Dave Aron and Andrew Rowsell-Jones, "Get Real: The Future of IT Infrastructure," Research Report (Stamford, CT: Gartner Executive Programs, December 2004).

3. This information about Celanese comes from unpublished interviews by George Westerman in 2004 and 2005 with Karl Wachs and other members of the company's IT senior management team. Summary information and quotes are included in "IT Risk Management: Four CIO Vignettes," video (Cambridge, MA: Center for Information Systems Research, MIT Sloan School of Management, 2005).

Chapter 3

1. ChipCo is a pseudonym.

2. Dave Aron and Andrew Rowsell-Jones, "Get Real: The Future of IT Infrastructure," Research Report (Stamford, CT: Gartner Executive Programs, December 2004).

3. Ibid.

4. Robert Ridout, global CIO, DuPont, interview by Richard Hunter, tape recording, July 11, 2006.

5. Jim Barrington, interview by George Westerman and Peter Weill, in Peter Weill et al., "Effective IT Oversight: Experienced CIOs Comment," video (Cambridge, MA: Center for Information Systems Research, MIT Sloan School of Management, 2005).

6. The IT risk pyramid has been published in various stages of refinement in Richard Hunter, George Westerman, and Dave Aron, "IT Risk Management: A Little Bit More Is a Whole Lot Better," Research Report (Stamford, CT: Gartner Executive Programs, February 2005); George Westerman, "The IT Risk Pyramid: Where to Start with Risk Management," Research Briefing V(1D) (Cambridge, MA: Center for Information Systems Research, MIT Sloan School of Management, March 2005); and George Westerman, "IT Risk Management: From IT Necessity to Strategic Business Value," working paper 366, Center for Information Systems Research, MIT Sloan School of Management, Cambridge, MA, December 2006.

7. "Case Studies in Crisis Management: How Wal-Mart, FedEx and Home Depot Got the Job Done," *Fortune*, September 21, 2005.

8. Roberta Witty, "Business Continuity Management Today: From Hurricanes to Blackouts to Terrorism" (paper presented at Gartner IT Security, Washington, DC, June 5–7, 2006).

9. Ibid.

10. Chuck Tucker and Richard Hunter, "September 11: Business Continuity Lessons," Research Report (Stamford, CT: Gartner Executive Programs, May 2002).

11. Several firms we interviewed mentioned that they outsource their IT operations because their vendor can provide disaster recovery more cheaply and effectively than they could on their own.

12. Tucker and Hunter, "September 11."

13. Vipul Shah and Manishwar Singh, phone interview by George Westerman, tape recording, October 26, 2005.

14. Bob Sullivan, "Huge Identity Theft Ring Busted—Help-Desk Worker Alleged Point Man in Theft of 30,000 IDs," with the Associated Press, MSNBC.com, November 25, 2002, http://www.msnbc.msn.com/id/3078518/.

15. John Pescatore and Avivah Litan, "Data Protection Is Less Costly Than Data Breaches," Research Note G00130911 (Stamford, CT: Gartner, September 16, 2005).

16. Ibid.

17. David Colker and Joseph Menn, "ChoicePoint Had Earlier Data Leak," *Los Angeles Times*, March 2, 2005.

18. These do not include eighteen major "application controls" (including such elements as data origination/authorization controls, data input controls, data-processing controls, data output controls, and boundary controls) because, as COBIT 4.0 puts it, "[t]he operational management and control responsibility for application controls is not with IT, but with the business process owner." See COBIT 4.0, available at http://www.isaca.org/.

19. ITIL is available at http://www.itil.co.uk. ISO 17799 is available at http://www.iso.org.

20. PricewaterhouseCoopers and IT Governance Institute, "IT Governance Global Status Report—2006," http://www.isaca.org/AMTemplate.cfm?Section=ITGI_Research_Publications&Template=/ContentManagement/ContentDisplay.cfm&ContentID=24224.

21. Richard Hunter and Matt Light, "Methodology and Productivity Study: The Data," Research Note SPA-480-1505 (Stamford, CT: Gartner, June 27, 1997); Richard Hunter and Matt Light, "Methodology and Productivity Study: The Analysis," Research Note SPA-480-1506 (Stamford, CT: Gartner, June 27, 1997).

Chapter 4

1. Dale Buss, "Nightmare," *Context Magazine*, Spring 1998.

2. George Westerman, Mark Cotteleer, Robert Austin, and Richard Nolan, "Tektronix, Inc.: Global ERP Implementation," Case 9-699-043 (Boston: Harvard Business School, 1999); Robert D. Austin, "Tektronix, Inc.: Global ERP Implementation," Teaching Note 5-602-078 (Boston: Harvard Business School, 2001); and Tektronix Annual Reports from 1999–2001.

3. Ibid.

4. Richard Ross, CIO, Amerada Hess, interview by Richard Hunter, adapted from Richard Hunter and Dave Aron, "From Value to Advantage: Exploiting Information," Research Report (Stamford, CT: Gartner Executive Programs, June 2004).

5. Information and quotations related to HUD are from Lisa Schlosser, CIO, HUD, interview by Richard Hunter, adapted from Richard Hunter and Dave Aron, "High Value, High Risk: Managing the Legacy Portfolio," Research Report (Stamford, CT: Gartner Executive Programs, September 2006).

6. Adapted from Hunter and Aron, "High Value, High Risk."

7. Ibid.

8. Westerman et al., "Tektronix, Inc."; Austin, "Tektronix, Inc." Teaching Note; and Tektronix Annual Reports from 1999–2001.

9. Adapted from Hunter and Aron, "High Value, High Risk."

10. Information and quotations related to Amerada Hess were from Richard Ross, CIO, Amerada Hess, interview by Richard Hunter, adapted from Hunter and Aron, "From Value to Advantage."

11. A *data mart* is an application that combines and reconciles information from multiple sources, usually for reporting and analysis purposes.

12. This section is adapted from Hunter and Aron, "High Value, High Risk."

13. Rob Pyne, CIO, Amcor, interview by Richard Hunter, in Hunter and Aron, "High Value, High Risk."

14. Information and quotations regarding FAIT Canada come from Pierre Sabourin, CIO, FAIT Canada, interview by Richard Hunter, in Richard Hunter and Dave Aron, "High Value, High Risk."

Chapter 5

1. Information in this section comes from George Westerman and Robert Walpole, "PFPC: Building and IT Risk Management Competency," working paper 352, Center for Information Systems Research, MIT Sloan School of Management, Cambridge, MA, April 2005.

2. We have seen the lines arranged effectively in both ways in different organizations. Some organizations do not have a corporate risk officer (or head of compliance or other related field). In those cases, the IT risk officer usually reports to the CIO.

3. Information about PFPC comes from Westerman and Walpole, "PFPC."

4. In most businesses, however, including large financial services businesses such as PFPC, it would be unusual for an IT risk to top the list, given the huge potential impact of, for example, credit or market risks. Having said that, it is not unusual to have IT risk near the top during a major IT transformation. In two firms we studied, IT transformation risk was among the top five enterprise risks that were reviewed regularly by the corporate board.

5. Richard Hunter, George Westerman, and Dave Aron, "IT Risk Management: A Little Bit More Is a Whole Lot Better," Research Report (Stamford, CT: Gartner Executive Programs, February 2005). A *risk register* is an ongoing record of risks and

their status. It records all identified risks so that they can be compared and monitored and ensures that the status of a risk can be retrieved at any time with minimal effort. In other words, the risk register is the enterprise's formal memory of risks and associated plans. As such, it is an important tool to enable an effective risk governance process. We discuss risk registers in more detail later in this chapter.

6. Tom Prince, multiple phone and in-person interviews by George Westerman, tape recording, Portsmouth, NH, February 2, 2004, and Cambridge, MA, 2004–2006.

7. We have spoken to many risk managers who have experimented with more complex methodologies, such as Monte Carlo analysis, but we haven't spoken to anyone who has found such approaches to be worth the time and effort beyond assessing risks in project management.

8. Stephanie Overby, "Bound to Fail," *CIO*, May 1, 2005; and Bob Driehaus, "How It Happened: Onslaught Overtaxed an Old Computer," *Cincinnati Post*, December 28, 2004.

9. Richard Hunter and Kristen Noakes-Frye, "Case Study: Information Security Governance at TeliaSonera," Research Note G00136835 (Stamford, CT: Gartner, February 28, 2006).

10. Review leadership rotates among members of TeliaSonera's cooperation team, the implementation level of its IT risk governance structure.

11. TeliaSonera's cooperative approach is further backed by a structured escalation process for handling exceptions to policy, so cooperation is not the only tool for ensuring compliance to policy.

12. Information and quotations presented here about PFPC come from Westerman and Walpole, "PFPC."

Chapter 6

1. A typical phishing attack is launched via an urgent e-mail purporting to be from a bank, eBay, Paypal, or another well-known business and requests that recipients log into a Web site and enter their ID, password, and other sensitive information. The Web site is a fake and operated by criminals seeking to steal personal information for profit. See Susannah Fox, *Spyware* (Washington, DC: Pew Internet & American Life Project, July 6, 2005).

2. Amy Edmondson, "Psychological Safety and Learning Behavior in Work Teams," *Administrative Science Quarterly* 44, no. 2 (1999): 350–383.

3. Don Peppers and Martha Rogers, "The New ChoicePoint: A Privacy Success Story," *Inside 1to1: Privacy*, December 14, 2006.

4. All material for this case is based on interviews in Dallas, TX, by George Westerman with Karl Wachs and other members of the Celanese management team, supplemented by Scott Berinato, "A Day in the Life of Celanese's Big ERP Rollup," *CIO*, January 15, 2003. The corresponding quotations from Karl Wachs are included in "IT Risk Management: Four CIO Vignettes," video (Cambridge, MA: Center for Information Systems Research, MIT Sloan School of Management, 2005).

5. Patrick Purcell, multiple interviews by George Westerman, 2003–2006. The quotations are included in "IT Risk Management: Four CIO Vignettes."

6. Information for this case study comes from Janet Nudds, interviews by Richard Hunter, March 2003, and with John Goddard, e-services global security manager, BOC, interviews by Richard Hunter, October 2004, as originally published in Richard Hunter, "IT Risk Management: The Office of the CIO Action Plan," Research Report (Stamford, CT: Gartner, December 2006).

7. The choice of project risk was a sensible first target for IT risk management. Gartner research shows that the typical IT organization spends close to 20 percent of its development resources on failed projects, and a simple program aimed at discovering early whether projects lack one or more of a handful of critical success factors can reduce that waste by 50 percent or more. See Richard Hunter, George Westerman, and Dave Aron, "IT Risk Management: A Little Bit More Is a Whole Lot Better," Research Report (Stamford, CT: Gartner Executive Programs, February 2005).

8. BOC Group Annual Report 2003.

Chapter 7

1. Royal Bank of Canada Annual Report 2004 (available at http://www.rbc.com /investorrelations/ar_04.html.

2. Bob Tedeschi, "Privacy Is Common Issue Online," *New York Times*, June 3, 2002.

3. EquipCo is a pseudonym.

4. PartCo is a pseudonym.

5. Research on IT governance has shown that this is the single most powerful indicator of a successful IT governance arrangement. See Peter Weill and Jeanne Ross, *IT Governance: How Top Performers Manage IT Decisions Rights for Superior Results* (Boston: Harvard Business School Press, 2004).

6. Gartner, Inc. interview with Microsoft IT security team by Richard Hunter, May 2005.

7. Survey of Gartner Executive Programs membership in the United States, Europe/Middle East/Africa, and Asia Pacific regions, June 2005.

8. Paul Erbach, interview by Richard Hunter, in Richard Hunter, George Westerman, and Dave Aron, "IT Risk Management: A Little Bit More Is a Whole Lot Better," Research Report (Stamford, CT: Gartner Executive Programs, February 2005).

9. Hans-Henrik Mejloe, interview by Dave Aron, in Dave Aron and Patrick Meehan, "Driving Enterprise Agility," Research Report (Stamford, CT: Gartner Executive Programs, April 2005).

Chapter 8

1. Jess J. Holland, "ChoicePoint ID Thefts Prompt Hearings," Associated Press, February 24, 2005; and Tom Zeller Jr., "U.S. Settles with Company on Leak of Consumers' Data," *New York Times*, January 27, 2006.

2. On March 31, 2006, the House Energy and Commerce Committee unanimously approved the Data Accountability and Trust Act, also known as HR 4127. The bill requires organizations to inform those whose data is "acquired by an unauthorized person" in the event of a data breach "if there is a reasonable basis to conclude that there is a significant risk of identity theft." The bill also requires data brokers to establish security policies and requires audits of organizations that experience security breaches. See http://thomas.loc.gov/cgi-bin/query/z?c109:H.R.+4127.

Key provisions of the Personal Data Privacy and Security Act of 2005, sponsored by Senator Arlen Specter (R-PA), chairman of the Senate Judiciary Committee, and Senator Patrick Leahy (D-VT), the panel's ranking member, include (1) increasing criminal penalties for identity theft involving electronic personal data and for computer fraud involving personal data and (2) making it a crime to conceal a security breach involving personal data. In addition, enterprises must give individuals access to, and the opportunity to correct, any personal information held by data brokers; establish internal policies that protect such data and vet third parties hired to process that data; give notice to individuals and law enforcement when a breach involving sensitive personal data occurs; and other responsibilities. See http://leahy.senate.gov/press/200506/062905a.html.

3. "Some empirical data suggests that the frequency of going-private transactions has increased following the passage of Sarbanes-Oxley." Marc Morgenstern, Peter Nealis, and Kahn Kleinman, LPA, "Going Private: A Reasoned Response to Sarbanes-Oxley?" U.S. Securities and Exchange Commission, 2004, http://www.sec.gov/info/smallbus/pnealis.pdf. See Grant Thornton LLP, "Post Sarbanes-Oxley: Number of Public Companies Going Private Increases 30 Percent," December 15, 2003, http://www.grantthornton.com (this article notes a 30 percent increase in going-private transactions during the sixteen months immediately following the enactment of the act compared to the sixteen months immediately preceding it); David A. Stockton et al., "Going Private: The Best Option?" *National Law Journal*, June 23–30, 2003 (these authors cite a study by FactSet Mergerstat indicating that going-private deals as a percentage of mergers and acquisition transactions increased by approximately 23.7 percent from 2001 to 2002). See also Stephen Pounds, "Software Firm Grabs the Bootstraps," *Palm Beach Post*, December 29, 2003 (this article notes that ninety-five U.S. companies went private during the twelve-month period ending in July 2003 compared to seventy-five U.S. companies for the previous twelve-month period). But see Gregory R. Samuel and Sally A. Schreiber, *Going Private Transactions*, 40-SPG TEX. J. BUS. LAW 85, 88 (2004) (these authors observe that the number of going-private transactions decreased from 2002 to 2003). "Pretty much everything is making you scratch your head and ask, 'Why am I a public company?'" Pounds, "Software Firm Grabs the Bootstraps" (quoting Marc Morgenstern).

4. Emma Connors and Eric Johnson, "Banks Double Basel II Spending," *Australian Financial Review*, April 10, 2006.

5. Paul Erbach, interview by Tina Nunno, in Tina Nunno, Marcus Blosch, and Lily Mok, "Emerging Markets—A 'Lite' Touch," Research Report (Stamford, CT: Gartner Executive Programs, February 2006).

6. See, for example, http://www.bankofamerica.com/privacy/sitekey/, or click on the "Prevent Password Theft" tab at https://login.yahoo.com/config/login_verify2?&.src=ym.

7. Andrew Kantor, "Sony: The Rootkit of All Evil?" *USA Today*, November 17, 2005, http://usatoday.com/tech/columnist/andrewkantor/2005-11-17-sony-root kit_x.html; and Bruce Schneier, "Real Story of the Rogue Rootkit," Wired News, November 17, 2005, http://www.wired.com/news/privacy/0,1848,69601,00.html.

8. Richard Hunter, *World Without Secrets* (New York: Wiley, 2002).

9. Clive Thompson, "Google's China Problem (And China's Google Problem)," *New York Times Magazine*, April 23, 2006.

10. Information and quotations related to OSF HealthCare come from Michael Nausman, interview by Richard Hunter, in Richard Hunter and David Aron, "High Value, High Risk: Managing the Legacy Portfolio," Research Report (Stamford, CT: Gartner Executive Programs, September 2006).

Index

About the Authors

George Westerman is a research scientist in the Center for Information Systems Research at the MIT Sloan School of Management. He focuses on CIO-level topics such as risk management, innovation, and IT value. He uses rigorous academic methods with a practice-oriented focus to generate IT management advice for both IT and non-IT executives. His research has been published in numerous case studies, articles, book chapters, and industry reports.

George is also faculty chair for the MIT Sloan Executive Education course, "IT for the Non-IT Executive." Prior to earning his doctorate from Harvard Business School, he gained more than fifteen years of experience in information technology and management. He is a frequent speaker at industry and corporate events, and regularly advises organizations on IT management topics.

Richard Hunter is group vice president and research director in Gartner Executive Programs, where his recent work has focused on information security and IT risk management issues for CIOs. Hunter is the author of the acclaimed book *World Without Secrets* (Wiley, 2002). He is in much demand as a speaker and adviser.

Hunter was elected a Gartner Fellow in 2003. He holds a bachelor's degree in music from Harvard University. He is a world-class harmonica player who continues to compose and perform, and is the author of *Jazz Harp*, the world's best-selling method for jazz and rock harmonica players (Oak Publications, 1980).